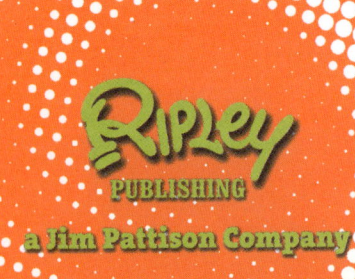

a Jim Pattison Company

Consultant Barbara Taylor
Design Rocket Design
Reprographics Juice Creative

Published by Ripley Publishing 2014
Ripley Publishing, Suite 188, 7576 Kingspointe Parkway
Orlando, Florida, 32819, USA

10 9 8 7 6 5 4 3 2 1

Copyright © 2014 by Ripley Entertainment, Inc.
All rights reserved. Ripley's, Believe It or Not!, and Ripley's Believe It or Not! are registered trademarks of Ripley Entertainment Inc.

ISBN 978-1-60991-116-4 (US)

Library of Congress Control Number: 2014939815

Manufactured in China
in June/2014
1st printing

PUBLISHER'S NOTE
While every effort has been made to verify the accuracy of the entries in this book, the Publishers cannot be held responsible for any errors contained in the work. They would be glad to receive any information from readers.

WARNING
Some of the stunts and activities in this book are undertaken by experts and should not be attempted by anyone without adequate training and supervision.

First published in Great Britain in 2014 by
Young Arrow, Random House,
20 Vauxhall Bridge Road, London SW1V 2SA

www.randomhouse.co.uk

Addresses for companies within The Random House Group Limited can be found at
www.randomhouse.co.uk/offices/htm

The Random House Group Limited Reg. No. 954009

A CIP catalogue record for this book is available from the British Library

ISBN 9780099596622 (UK)

No part of this publication may be reproduced in whole or in part, or stored in a retrieval system, or transmitted in any form or by any means, electronic, mechanical, photocopying, recording, or otherwise, without written permission from the publisher.

For information regarding permission, write to
VP Intellectual Property
Ripley Entertainment Inc.
Suite 188, 7576 Kingspointe Parkway
Orlando, Florida, 32819, USA
Email: publishing@ripleys.com
www.ripleybooks.com

Pretty in pink

In the doghouse!

Believe it or not, these houses are for dogs!

Some of them even have air conditioning and running water!

Now, where did I bury my bone?

Cheeky Monkey

Female baboons bring up their young alone.

B.F.F.

Six-year-old Emily Bland is best friends with Rishi the orangutan. They met when they were very young, and have stayed friends ever since.

TIGER FACTS

Tigers can kill prey over twice their size.

They have **striped skin,** as well as striped fur.

Tigers are the **largest wild cats** in the world.

SWEET DREAMS

A piglet sleeps with a tiger in a zoo in Bangkok, Thailand, where they have lived happily together from an early age.

Japan has roads that play music as you drive over them at the correct speed.

You can't hum while holding your nose. **Try it!**

Monster Munch?

Stuffed olive eyes

Tomato tongues

Salamiese Twins

BICYCLE SPECTACLE

The owners of a bicycle shop in Germany attached 120 bikes to the building to advertise their shop.

It measured 43,000 square feet (4,000 sq m)!

20

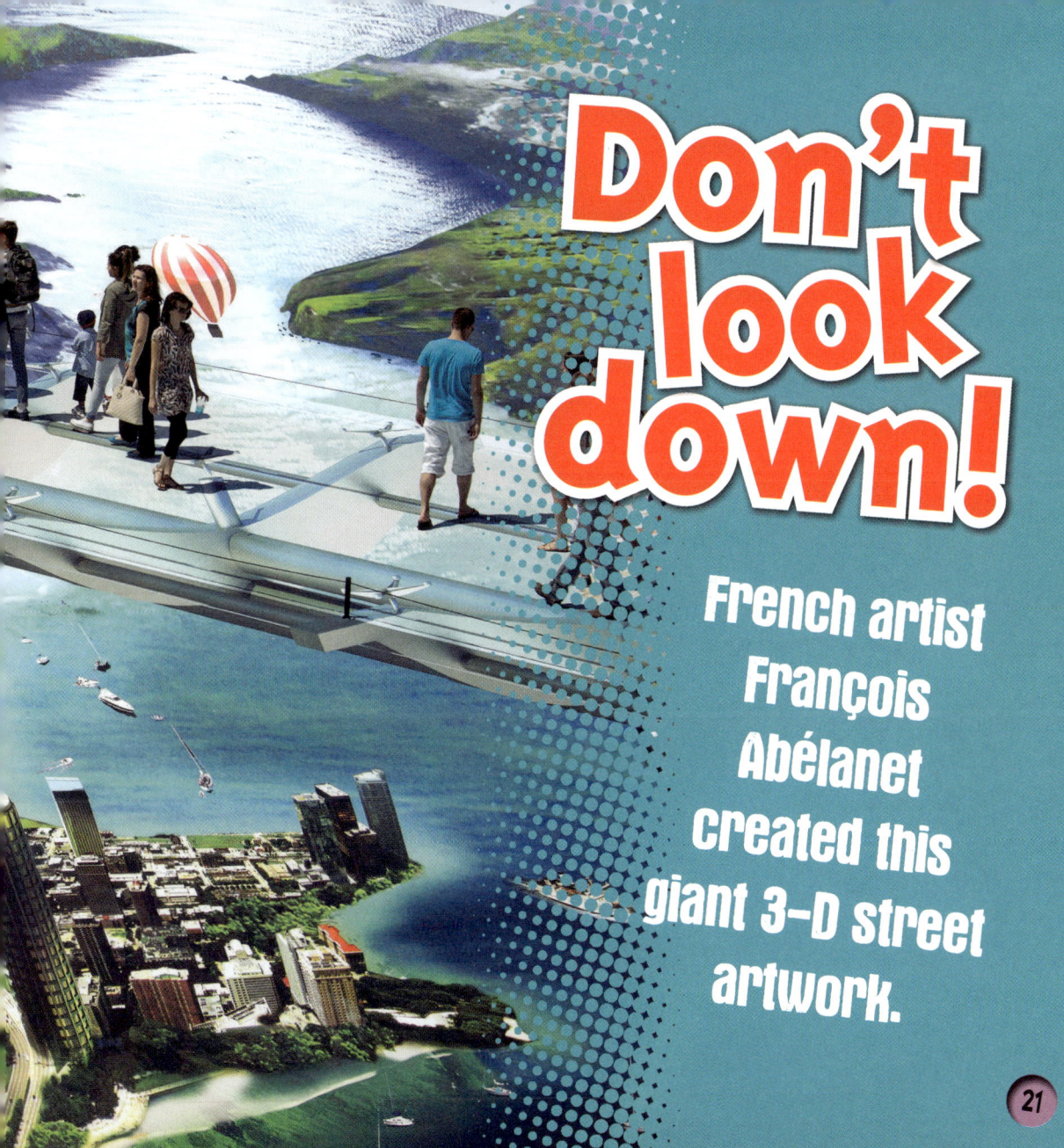

Don't look down!

French artist François Abélanet created this giant 3-D street artwork.

WEEE... SPLAT!

A farmer from Holland set up a slide for his muddy pigs!

Dull in Scotland is the sister town of **Boring** in Oregon.

Your brain is often more active when you are asleep than when you are awake.

FLYING FOOLS!

These crazy contestants have made their own aircraft for a flying competition. They jump from a platform into the sea, and the machine that travels the furthest wins!

The Fish

LOONY LOADS!

Have you ever tried carrying lots of things at once? Probably not as much as these heavy loads...

Phew, this cycling is thirsty work!

Plastic bottles on the back of a rickshaw in India.

Lanterns on the back of a motorcycle in Sri Lanka.

A sofa on the back of a motorcycle in Kenya.

TAXI!

Cats can't taste sweetness.

They do not have the sense organ for sweetness.

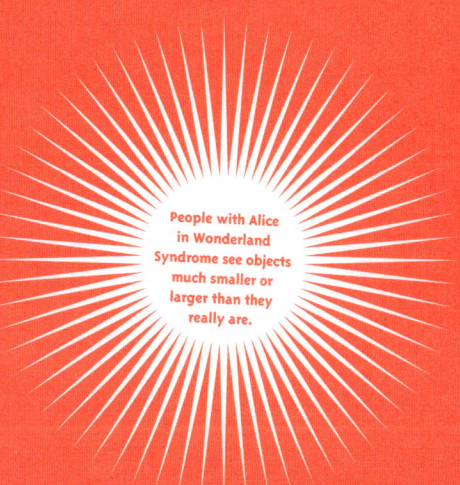

People with Alice in Wonderland Syndrome see objects much smaller or larger than they really are.

THAT'S POTTY!

Janey Byrne lives with her pot-bellied pigs, Molly and Meeka, in her home in the U.K.

It's crumbs again Meeka.

Er, waiter...

...there's a worm in my soup!

Earthworm soup is popular in China and is thought to cure fevers.

These cuddly mascots took part in the world's largest gathering of mascot characters in Japan.

The giant squid has the world's largest eyes. They are the size of a **dinner plate!**

Grrrrr!

Walt Disney, creator of Mickey Mouse, was afraid of mice!

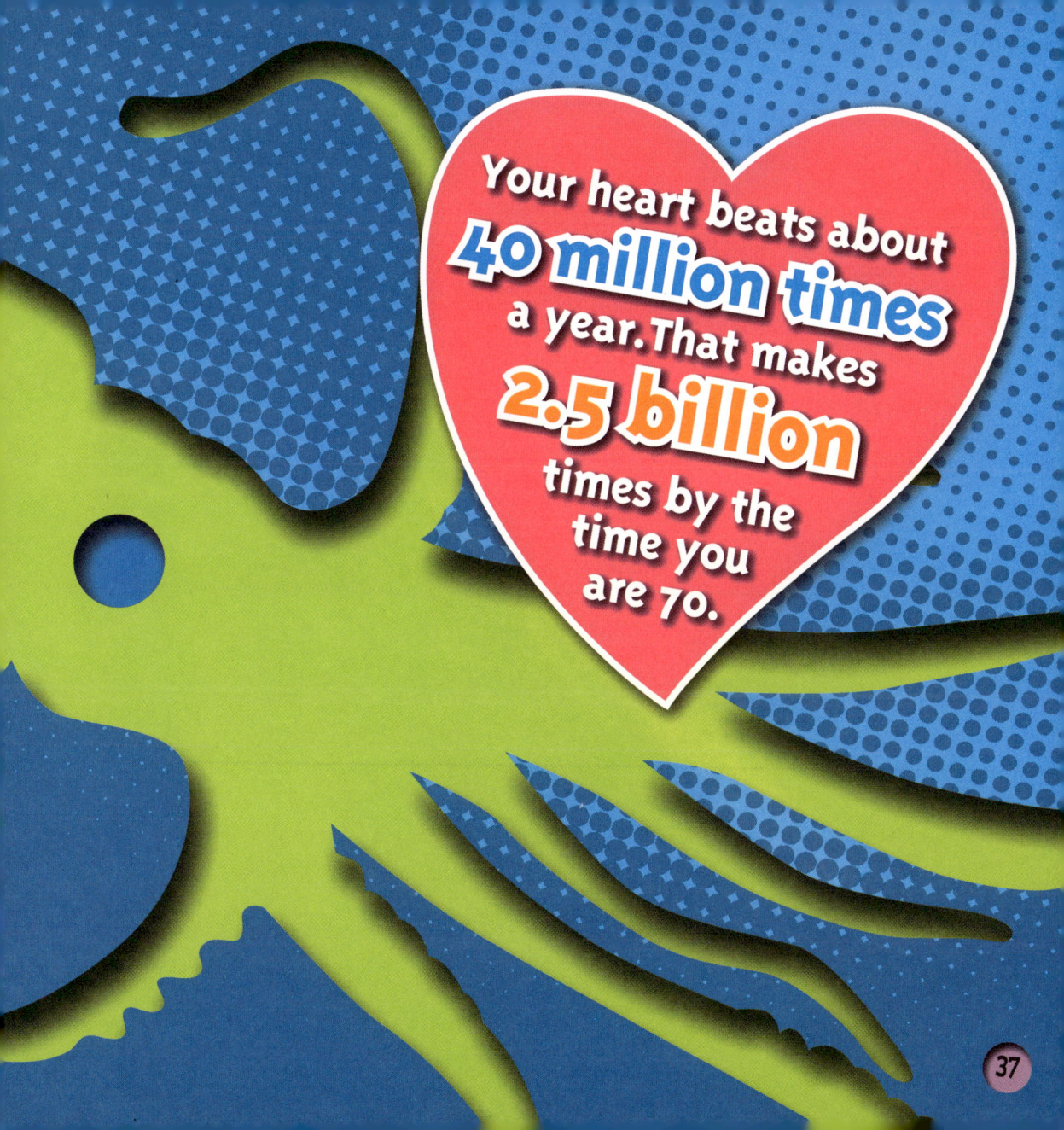

Your heart beats about **40 million times** a year. That makes **2.5 billion** times by the time you are 70.

This Hide-N-See TV for hamsters, gerbils and mice lets your pet star in its own TV show!

"I'm a celebrity, get me out of here!"

EYES ON THE PRIZE

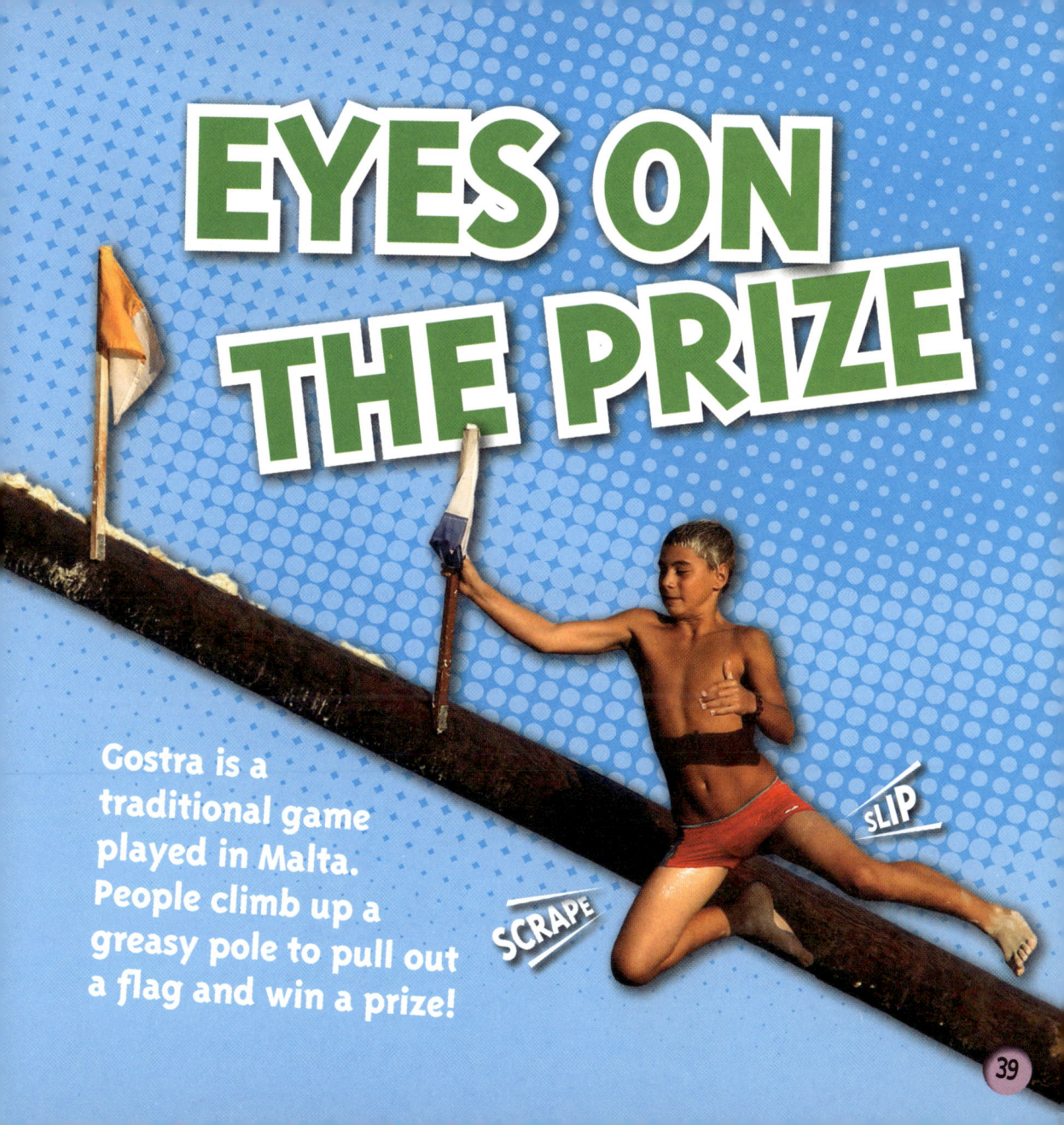

Gostra is a traditional game played in Malta. People climb up a greasy pole to pull out a flag and win a prize!

SCRAPE

SLIP

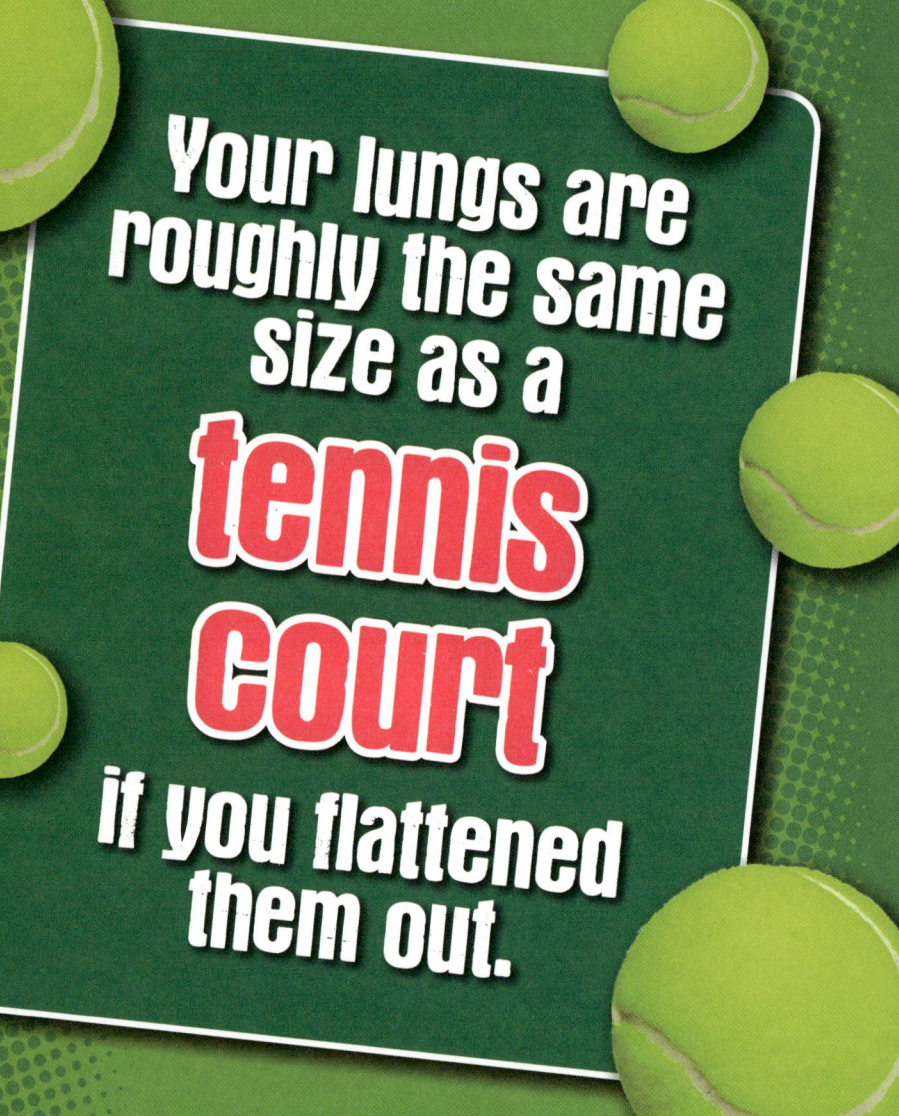

Your lungs are roughly the same size as a tennis court if you flattened them out.

THE APPLE OF MY EYE...

Special Valentine's Day apples featuring love messages were sold at a supermarket in China.

GENTLE JAWS

Mother crocodiles often carry their babies in their mouths after they have hatched so they reach the water safely.

Eeek, don't swallow me!

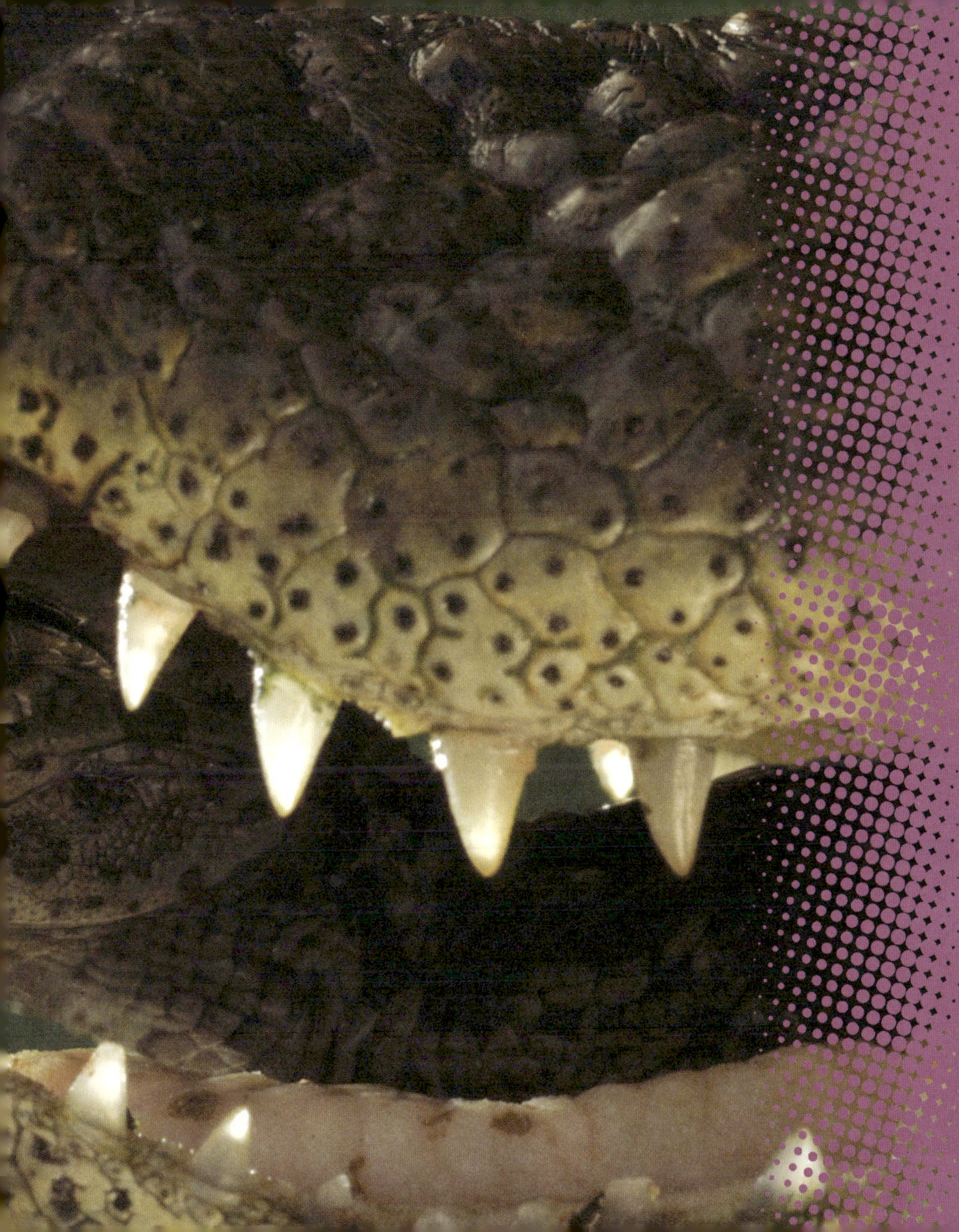

Tomatoes

Lettuce

Hand!

THE GREEN MAN

Can you spot him? Artist Liu Bolin hides in this store display by painting himself covered in vegetables.

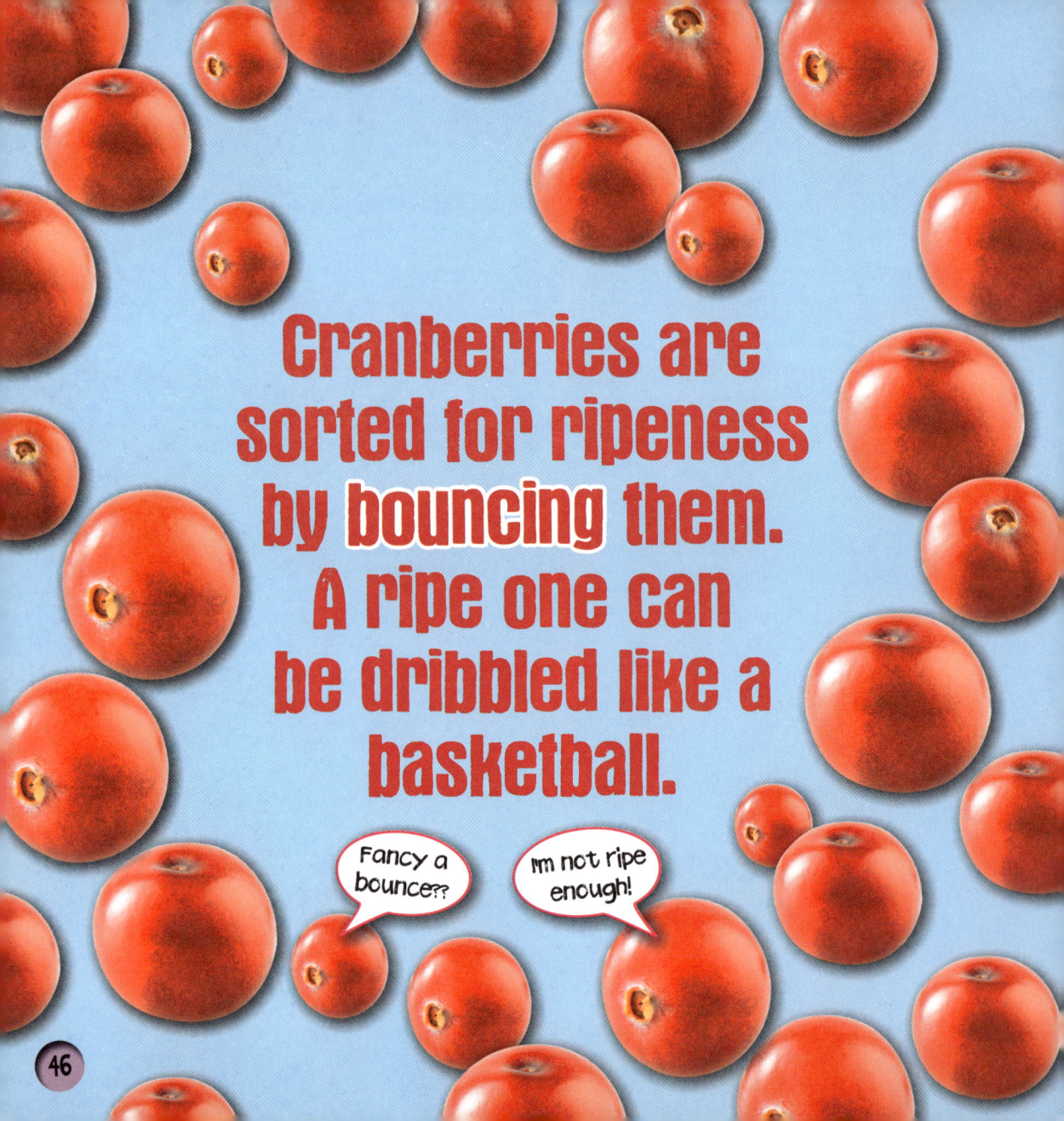

Cranberries are sorted for ripeness by **bouncing them.** A ripe one can be dribbled like a basketball.

Fancy a bounce??

I'm not ripe enough!

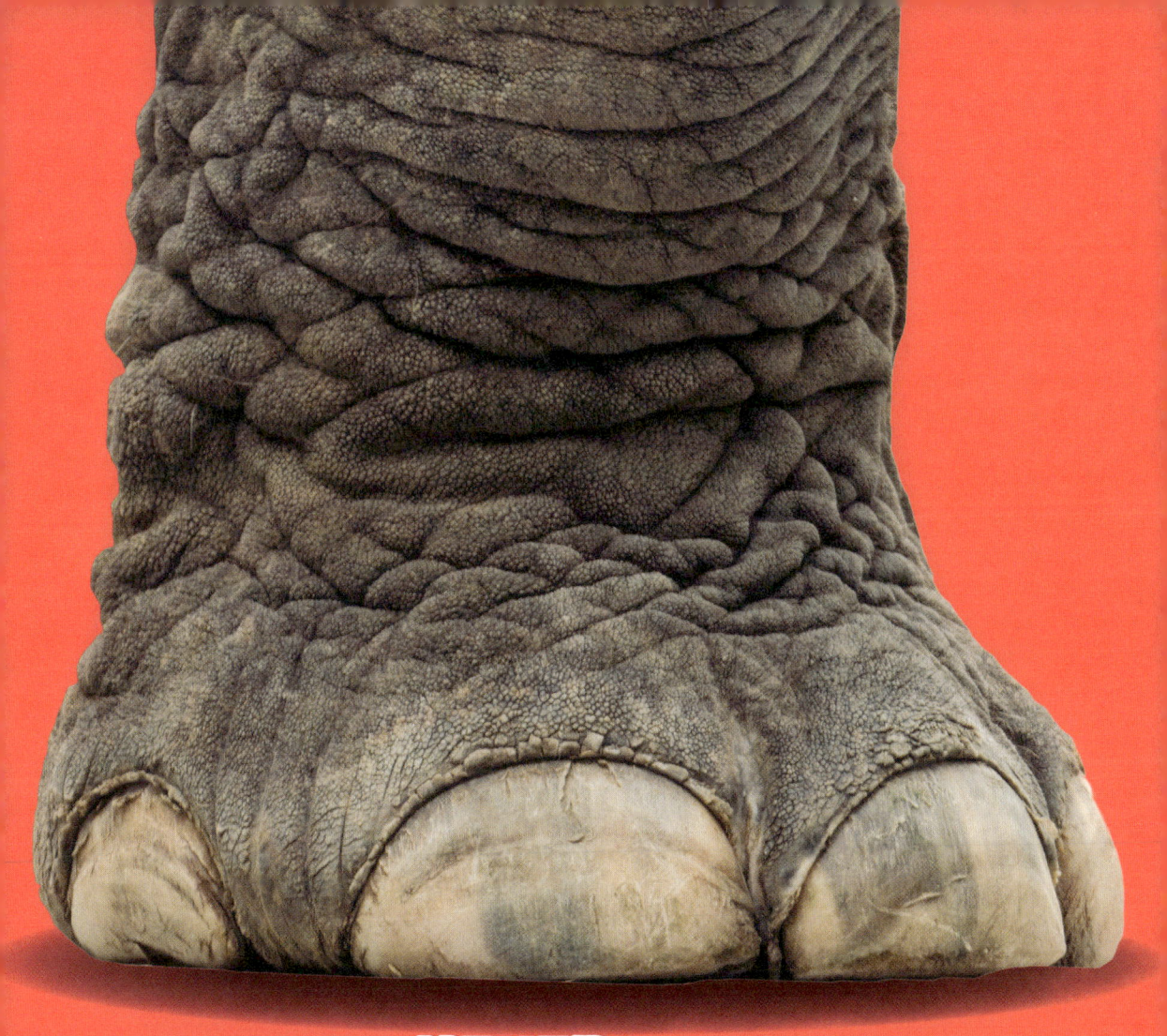

Elephants NEVER stop growing.

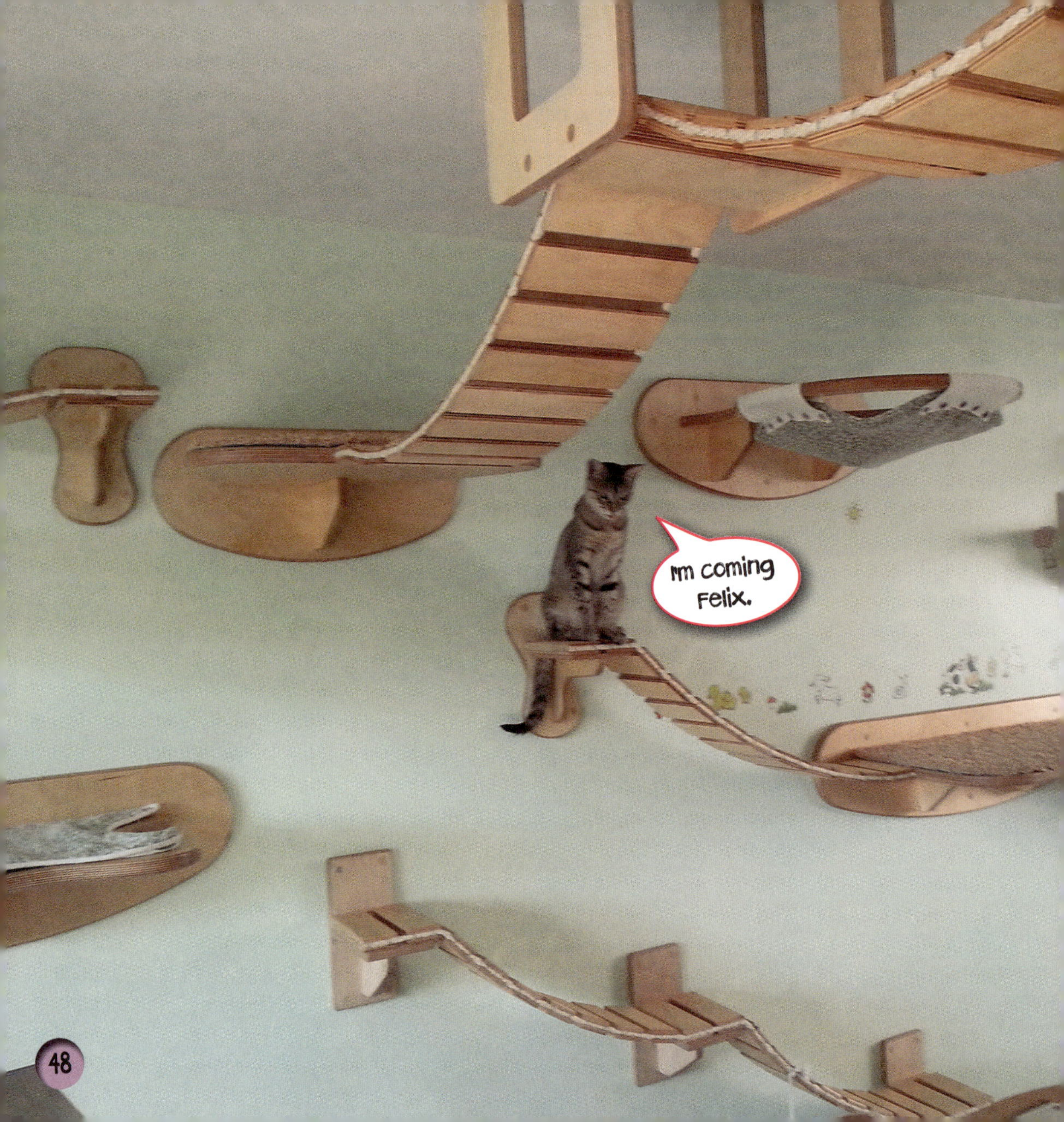
I'm coming Felix.

felineFUN

Check out this cool furniture for cats! They can explore the walkways and beds attached to the walls and ceilings.

That doesn't look very comfy!

Help me!

...AND BREATHE!

Gulp, wheeze!

PUFF, PANT! We've never gone down that deep before Billy-Bob!

Mudskippers, a type of fish, can drown underwater. They need to be able to poke their heads above the water to breathe.

51

BEST BUDS!

Grizzly bear cub Bam Bam and Vali the chimp are best buddies!

They live in Myrtle Beach Safari Park in South Carolina.

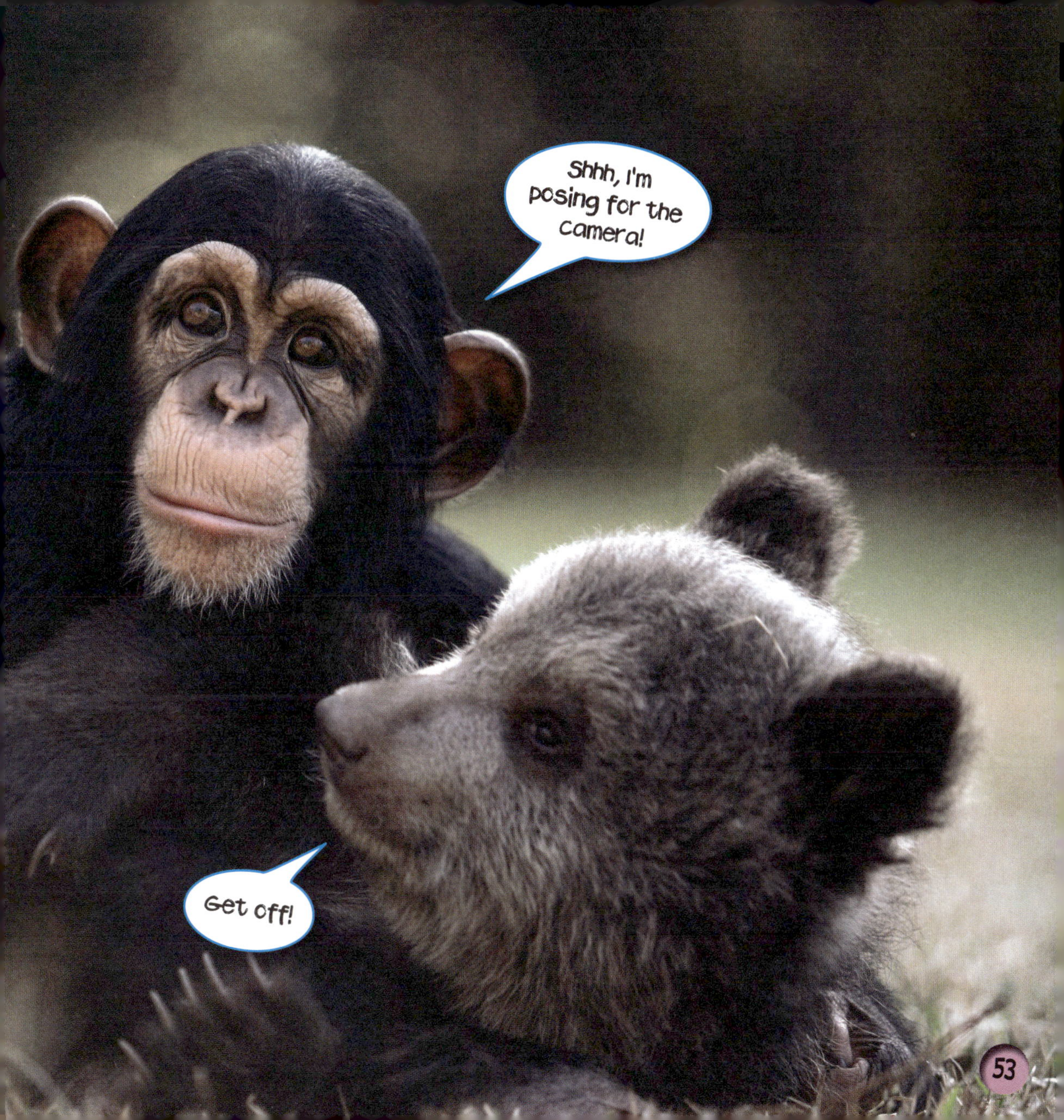
Shhh, I'm posing for the camera!
Get off!

SMILE!

This watermelon carving was made by a student in China using only a spoon.

Palm trees grew in Antarctica **50 million** years ago.

ANTS STRETCH when they wake up in the morning.

Little Miss Cuddly

Jo Black from the U.K. has 2,700 pieces in her Mr. Men and Little Miss collection.

Let me out!

57

ONION FACTS

If you rub an onion on your foot, within an hour **you will taste it.**

This is because it travels through your skin and into your bloodstream.

Eating onions will make you sleepy, but you'll have to eat a lot of them!

Chewing gum while peeling onions will stop you from crying.

TONGUE TALENT

Giant Anteaters' tongues are about two feet (0.6 m) long.

You'll have to take my word for it, it's rude to stick your tongue out!

The ancient Aztecs ate tortillas stuffed with **TADPOLES** for dinner.

Are you fur real?

Mohawk

Designer Leah Workman has created these wacky wigs for dogs!

Pink Wig

Blue 'do

Smokin'!

John Ward from the U.K. has created the world's smallest working fire truck!

An average person laughs **TEN** times a day.

"Strewth!"

There are more than 60 kinds of kangaroo.

The female black widow spider's poison is **15 times** deadlier than a rattlesnake's!

It took 10 million bricks to build the Empire State Building.

GULP!

In your lifetime you will drink enough water to fill 20 swimming pools.

So, by the time you are 80, you will have drunk over 1.5 million gallons (5.7 million l) of water.

GEEZER!

An elephant's trunk holds up to 2 gallons (10 l) of water.

Rats laugh when tickled

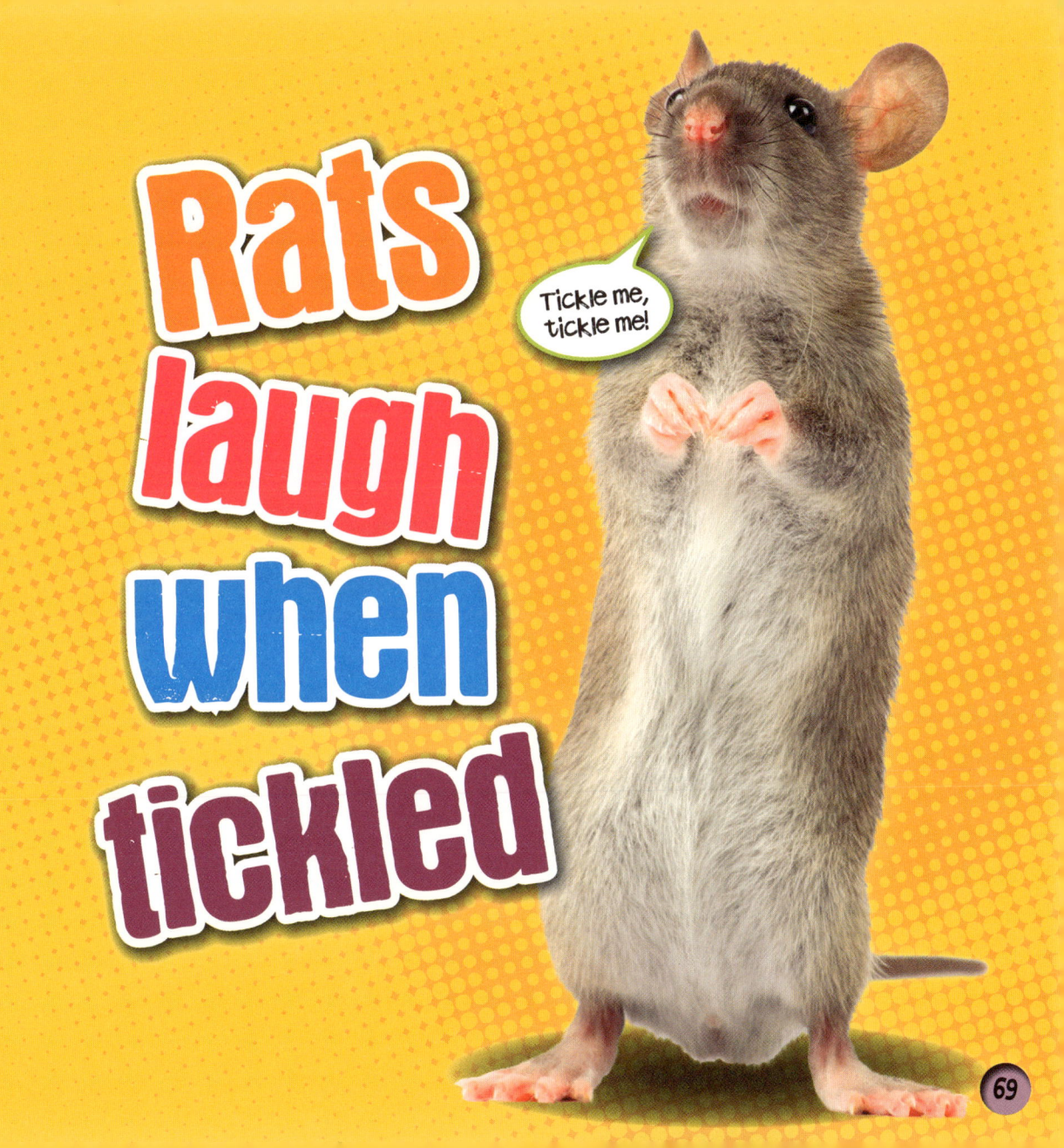

Tickle me, tickle me!

ONE tree produces enough oxygen in one year to keep **TWO** human beings alive.

Thanks.

You're welcome!

A bunch of bananas is called a **HAND.**

A single banana is known as a **FINGER.**

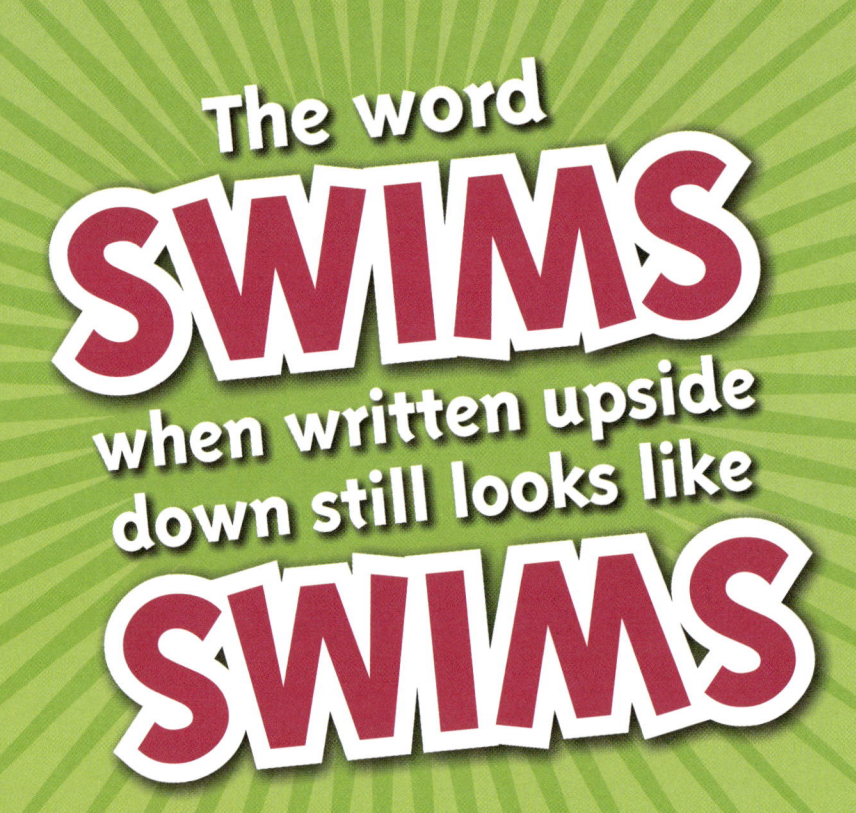

The word **SWIMS** when written upside down still looks like **SWIMS**

Most crabs grow a new claw when they lose one.

Do flying fish fly?

No, they just glide on wind currents. Some glide 20 feet (6 m) above the water.

I'm flying!

No, you're not!

Big-hearted beasts

A waterbuck with a heart-shaped nose!

A fluffy penguin with a heart-y chest.

A cat with a heart on its chin!

Rhys!
SCISSORS!

ROCK,

The Rock, Paper, Scissors Championships were held in the U.K. in 2013. Rhys Parkey beat 249 other competitors to be crowned champion.

NUTS!

PAPER, SCISSORS!

Some worms in Australia are over four feet (1.2 m) long!

Giant pandas spend up to 16 hours a day eating bamboo.

Why did a man wear **70 ITEMS** of clothing to a Chinese airport?

So he didn't have to pay the extra baggage charge!

RAISE

Is that you Linda?

Hey, watch it!

PERISCOPES!

Elephants can swim, and they use their trunk like a snorkel to breathe when they're in deep water.

I'm over here Brian!

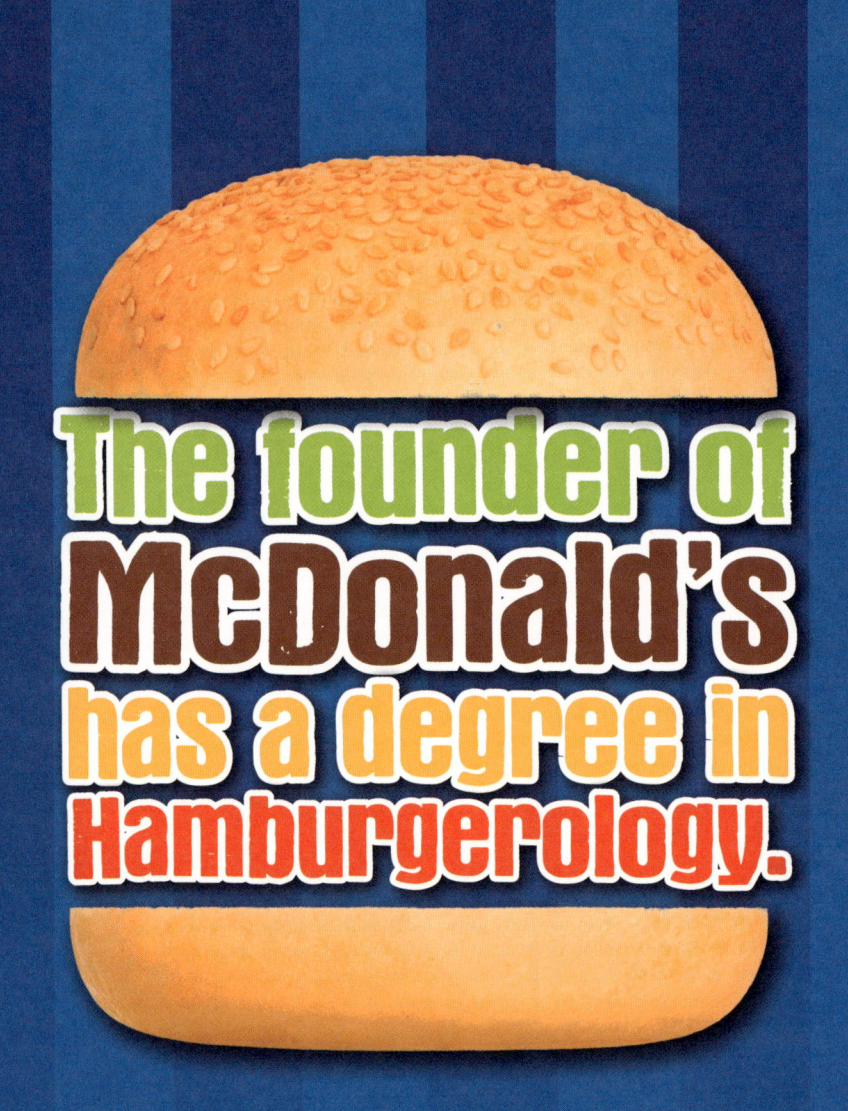

The founder of McDonald's has a degree in Hamburgerology.

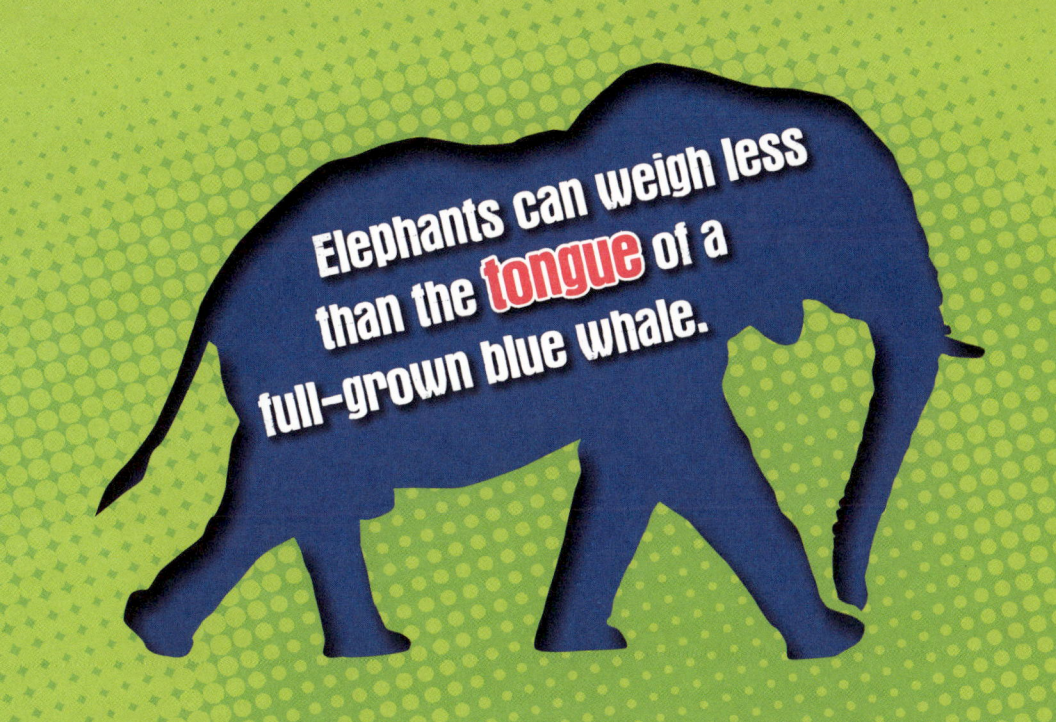

Elephants can weigh less than the *tongue* of a full-grown blue whale.

Horses can only breathe through their nostrils, not their mouth.

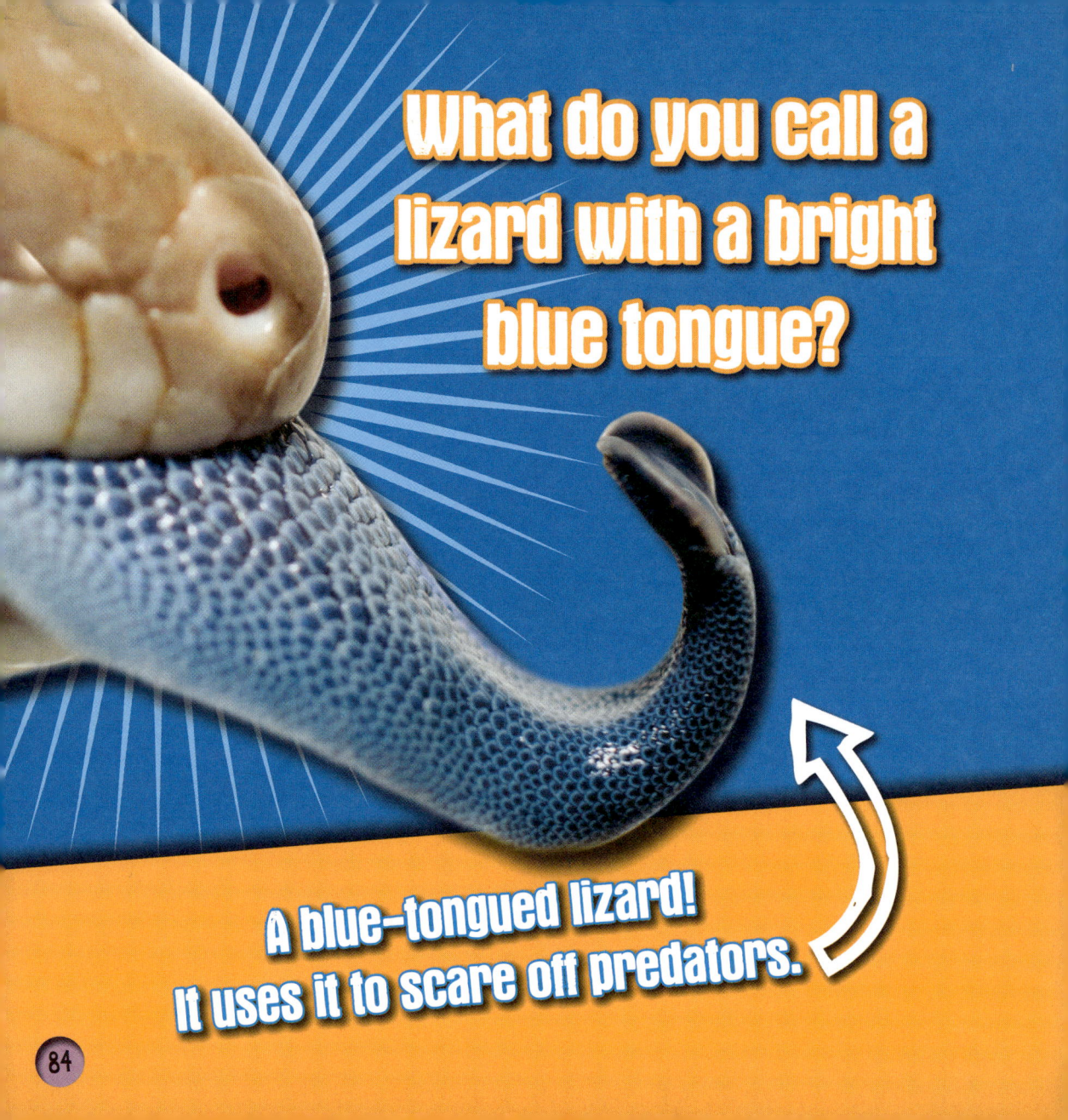

What do you call a lizard with a bright blue tongue?

A blue-tongued lizard! It uses it to scare off predators.

When you tell a lie your nose heats up.

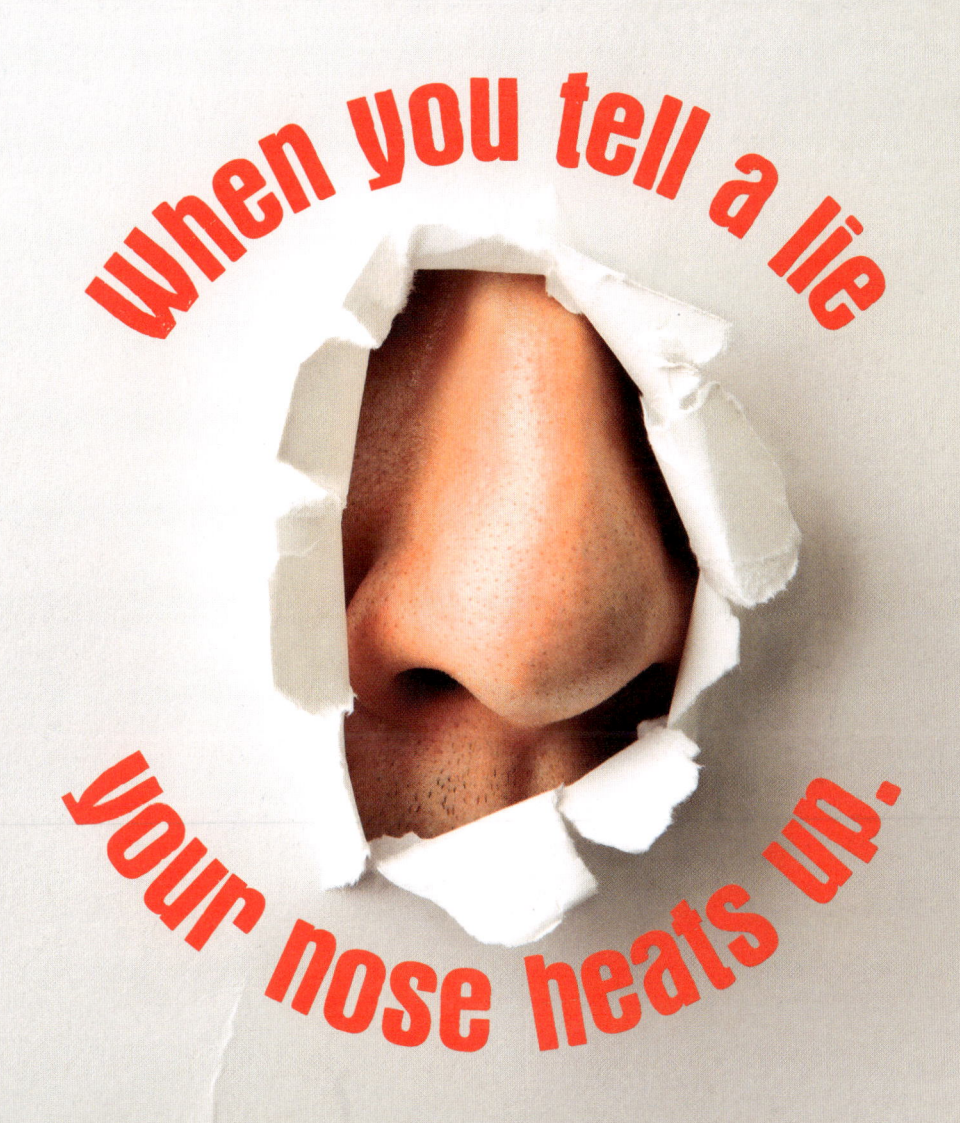

85

HORSES CAN SLEEP

STANDING UP!

It's getting late guys, we'd better "lock up" for the night.

They lock their knees so they don't fall over.

FISH SUPPER

A black swan feeds carp at a wildlife park in China.

BIG TANK!

A Boeing 747 airliner holds 57,285 gallons (216,847 l) of fuel.

Fill 'er up mate.

That may take some time sir!

Vending machines **kill 4 times more people** each year than sharks.

A group of bunnies is called a fluffle.

Did someone say carrots?

Gentoo and Adélie penguins give their mate a pebble as a way of proposing.

Popping the question

Hmmm, I'd rather have a ring!

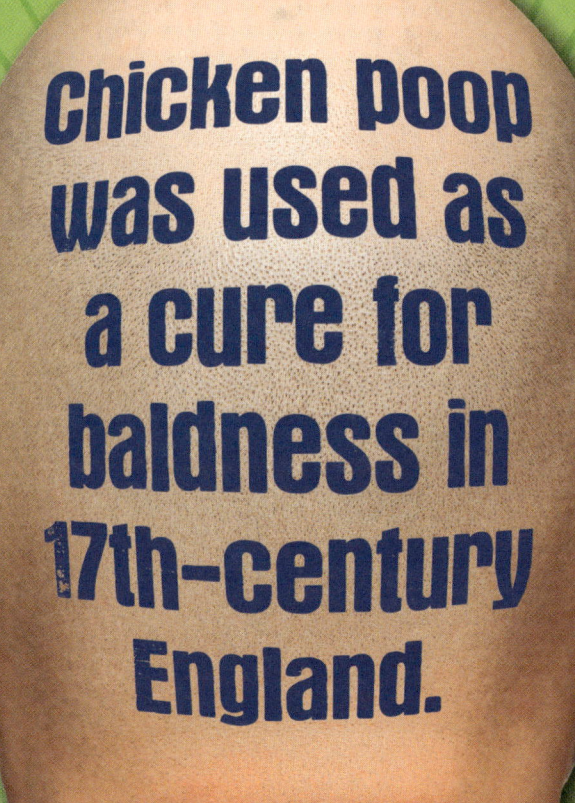

Chicken poop was used as a cure for baldness in 17th-century England.

Dogs are banned from Antarctica.

Santa Claus received nine votes in the 2008 U.S. presidential election.

It's almost **IMPOSSIBLE** to sneeze with your eyes open.

Hagfish have four hearts.

POP!

Believe it or not, this is what an exploding balloon full of water looks like! It was photographed by Shimon Mentel from Israel.

This is the world's biggest glass Christmas tree bauble!

It measures 65 inches (165 cm) across and weighs 44 pounds (20 kg).

Your left side is your best side

Scientists think people find it more attractive.

twyndyllyngs is the longest English word without a vowel. It's another word for "twin."

Astronauts get taller when they are in space.

They grow about 2 inches (5 cm) taller during long missions due to the lack of gravity that pulls them down on Earth. When they return home, they shrink back to normal.

Do sheep enter beauty contests?

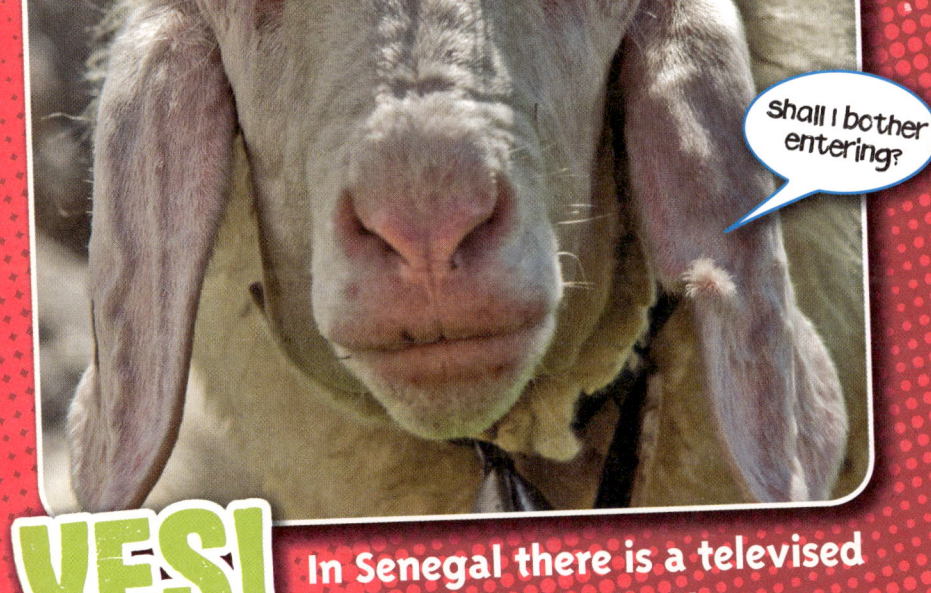

Shall I bother entering?

YES!

In Senegal there is a televised beauty contest for sheep.

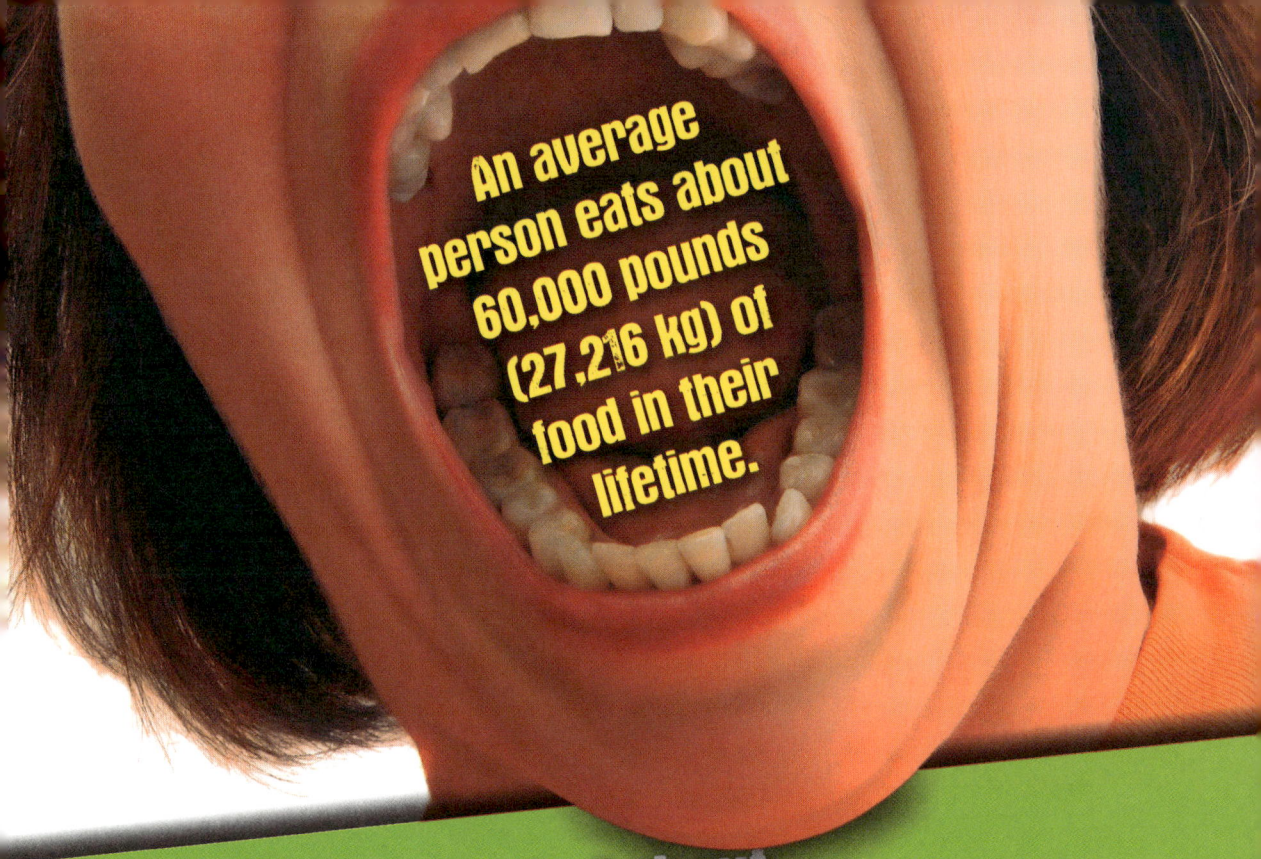

An average person eats about 60,000 pounds (27,216 kg) of food in their lifetime.

That's the weight of about **six elephants** or **30 small cars.**

Cows can be identified by their noseprints.

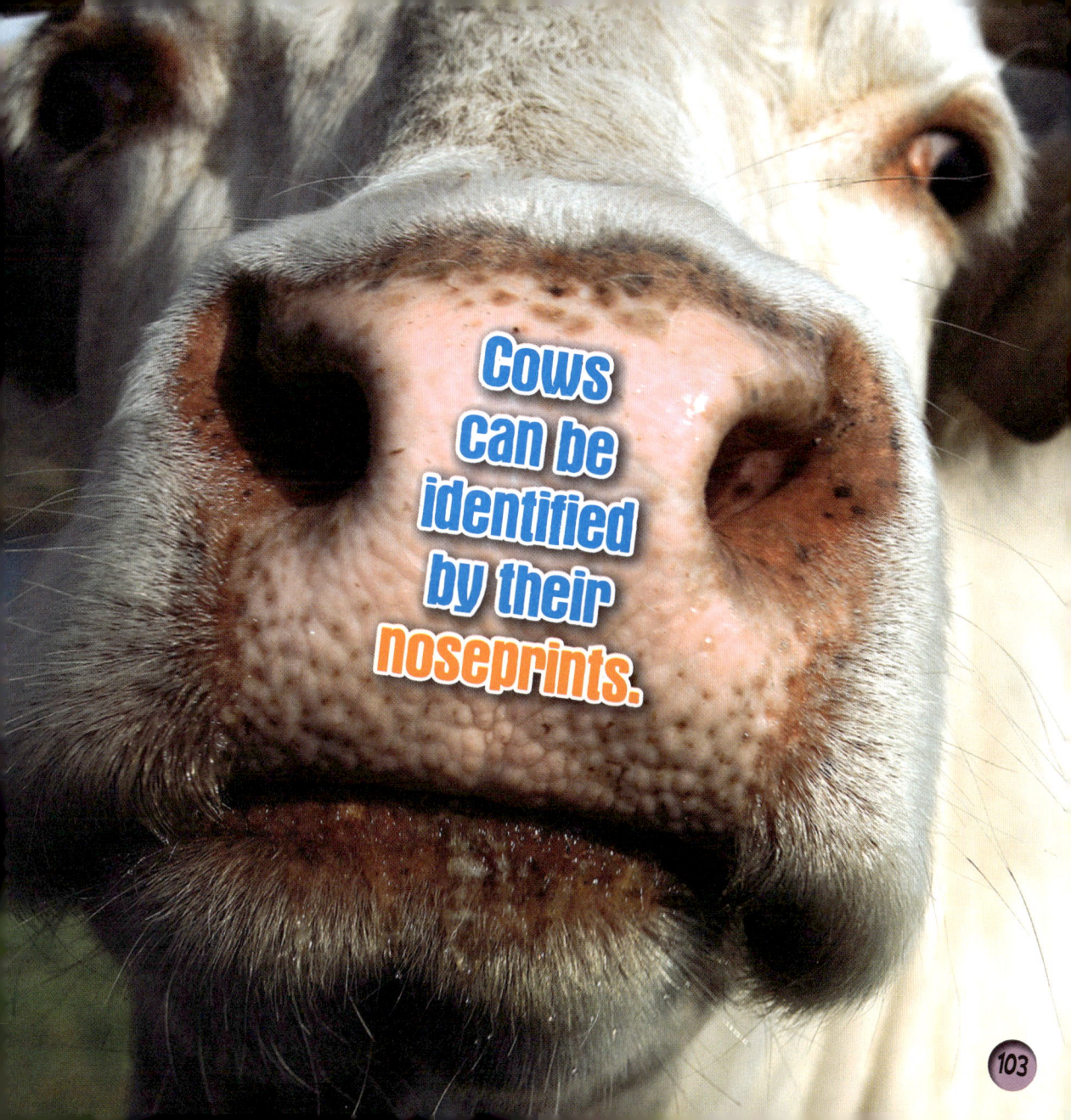

SMASH, POP, BOUNCE!

Bubble soccer is a sport played all over the world—it's the same as soccer but every player is inside an inflatable bubble!

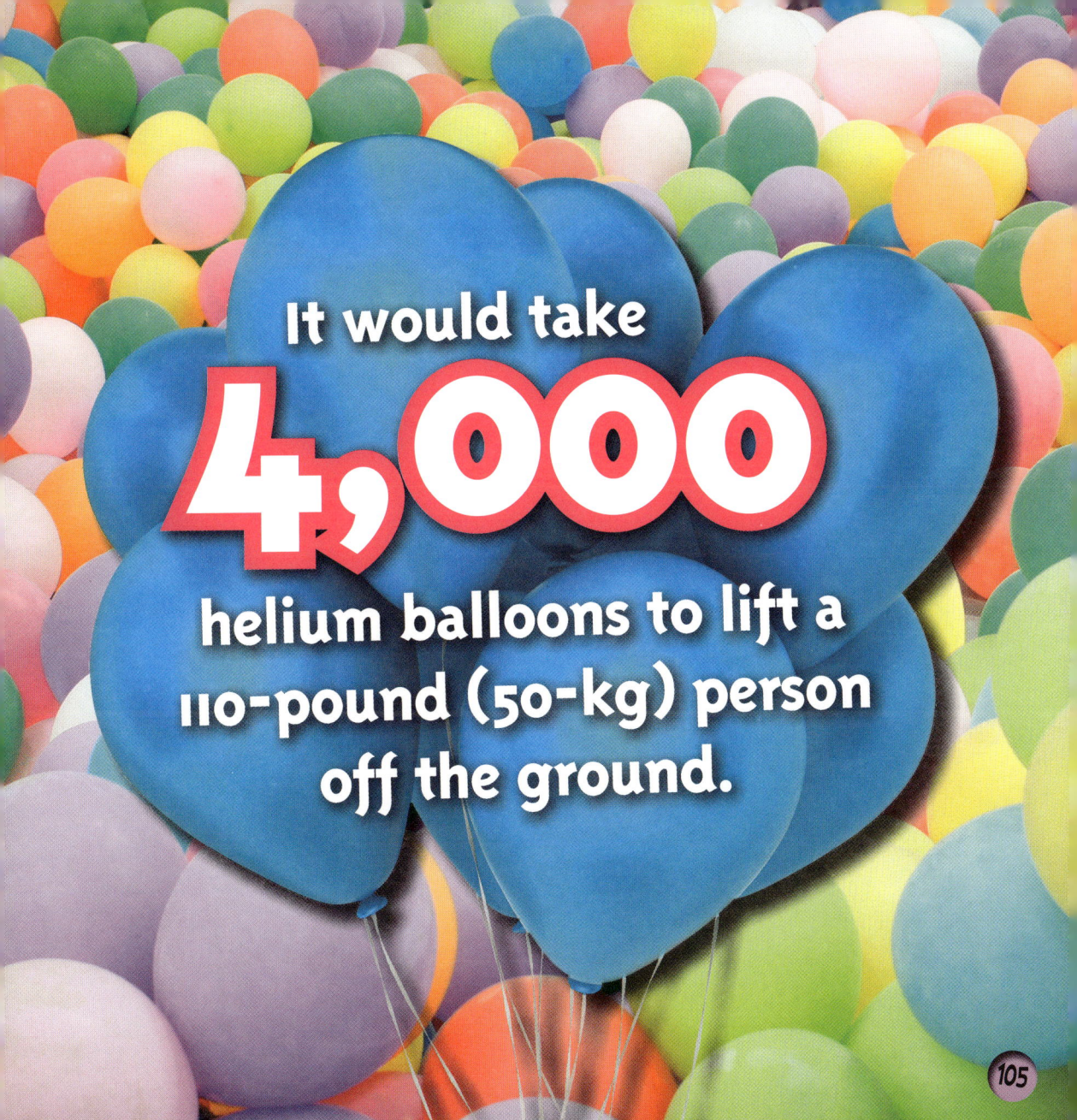

It would take **4,000** helium balloons to lift a 110-pound (50-kg) person off the ground.

DUCK SOUP!

12,000 rubber ducks took part in a duck race in Germany.

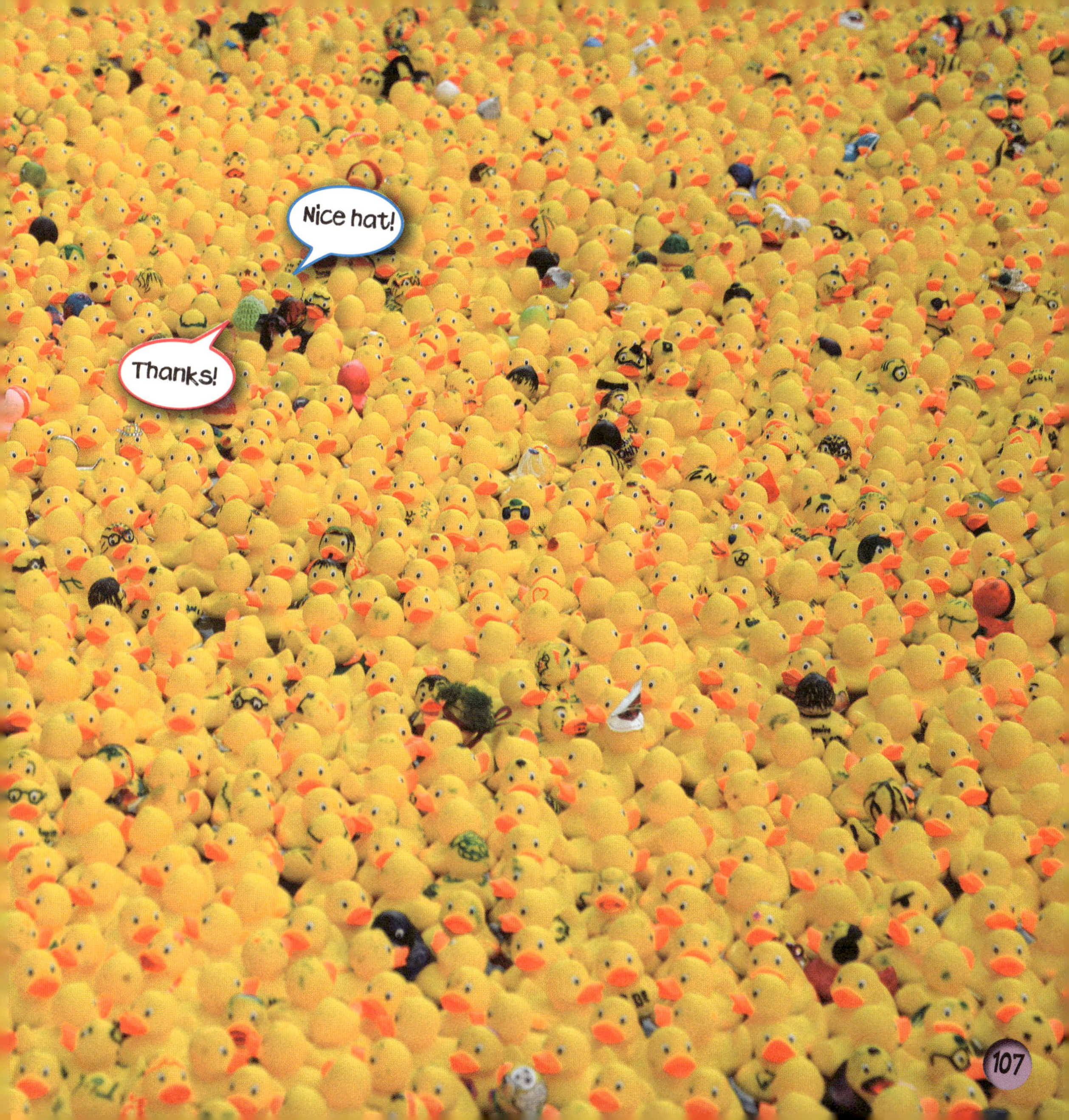
Nice hat!
Thanks!

The space between your eyebrows is called the **glabella.**

I wish I had some eyebrows.

Las Vegas would be the **BRIGHTEST** city if you looked down at Earth from space at night.

Night-flying tropical butterflies have **EARS** on their wings to avoid crashing into bats.

Lungfish can survive without water for as long as four years.

Scientists can't agree why ice is slippery.

Really?

The ultimate BRAIN FOOD!

Andy Millns made a miniature copy of his brain out of chocolate… and then ate it!

Astronauts in space often lose their sense of smell and taste.

Sorry!

Proot!

No problem Tony, I can't smell a thing.

Woodlice drink from both ends of their body.

ZZZZZZZZZZZ...
In Germany, there is a snoring museum.

One inch (2.5 cm) of rain =

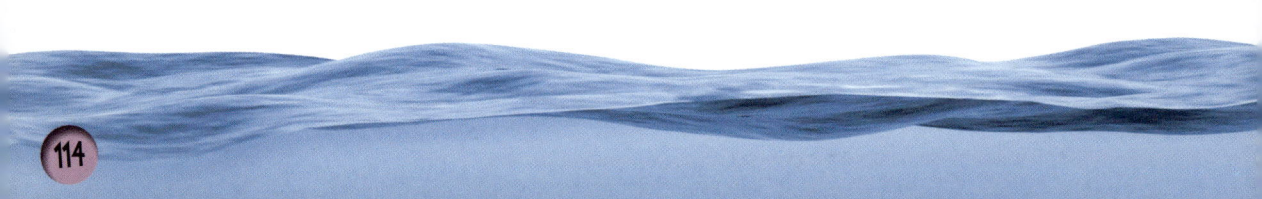

= **10 inches**
(25 cm)
of snow.

Winging it!

Dang! who stole my parking space?

Flying is the new way to get to work, with this flying bicycle. The bike can reach heights of up to 4,000 feet (1,200 m).

BANANA MAN

Humans and bananas share **50 percent** of the same genes.

EDIBLE ORGANS

Hand

Kidney

Eyes

Liver

118

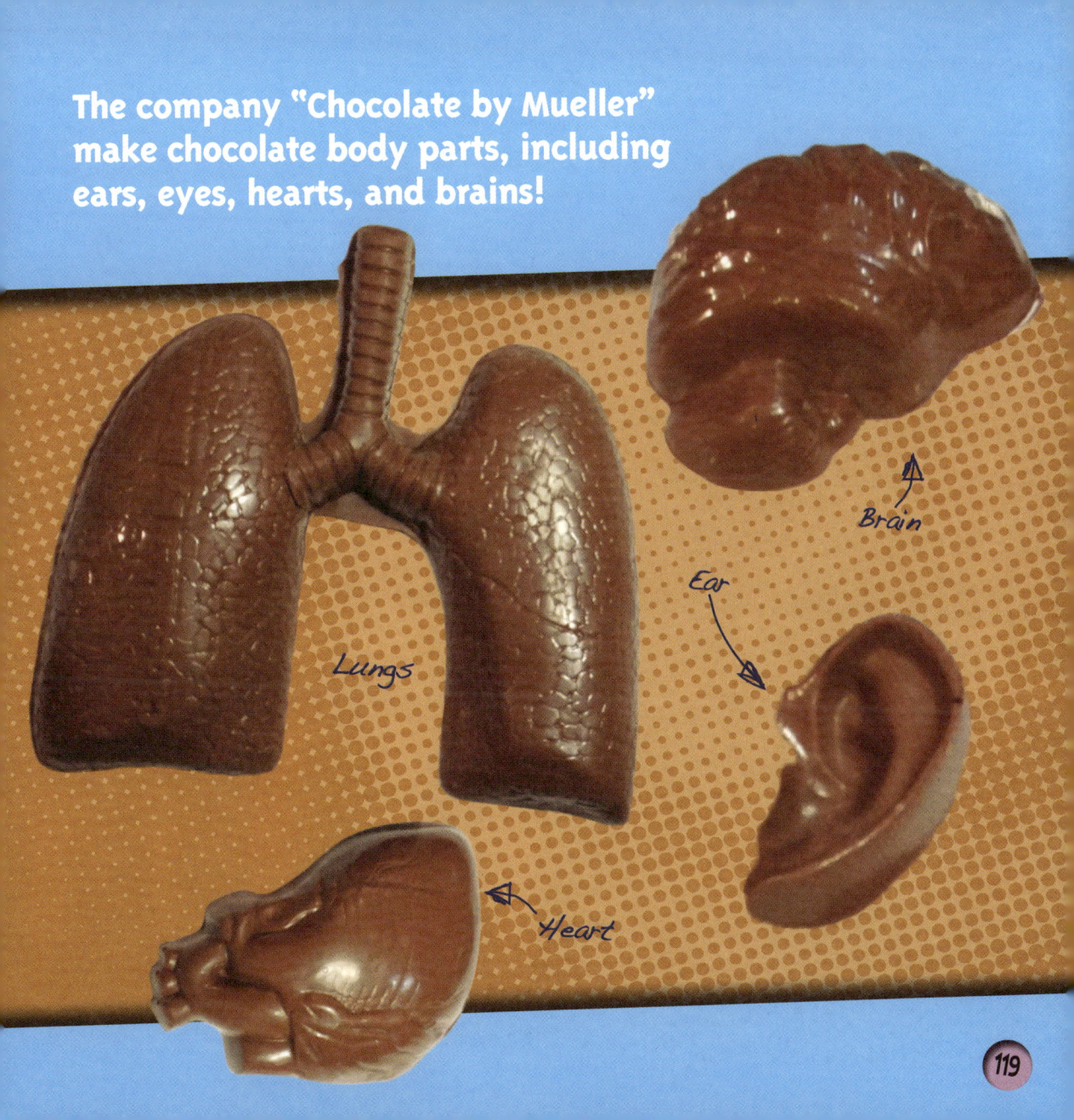

The company "Chocolate by Mueller" make chocolate body parts, including ears, eyes, hearts, and brains!

Lungs

Brain

Ear

Heart

119

Mosquito repellents don't repel, they actually hide your smell.

More than 30 million people in China live in CAVES.

BEST MATES

Cows have best friends and can get stressed when they are separated.

Ha, they won't separate us now Kate!

Is this a good idea?

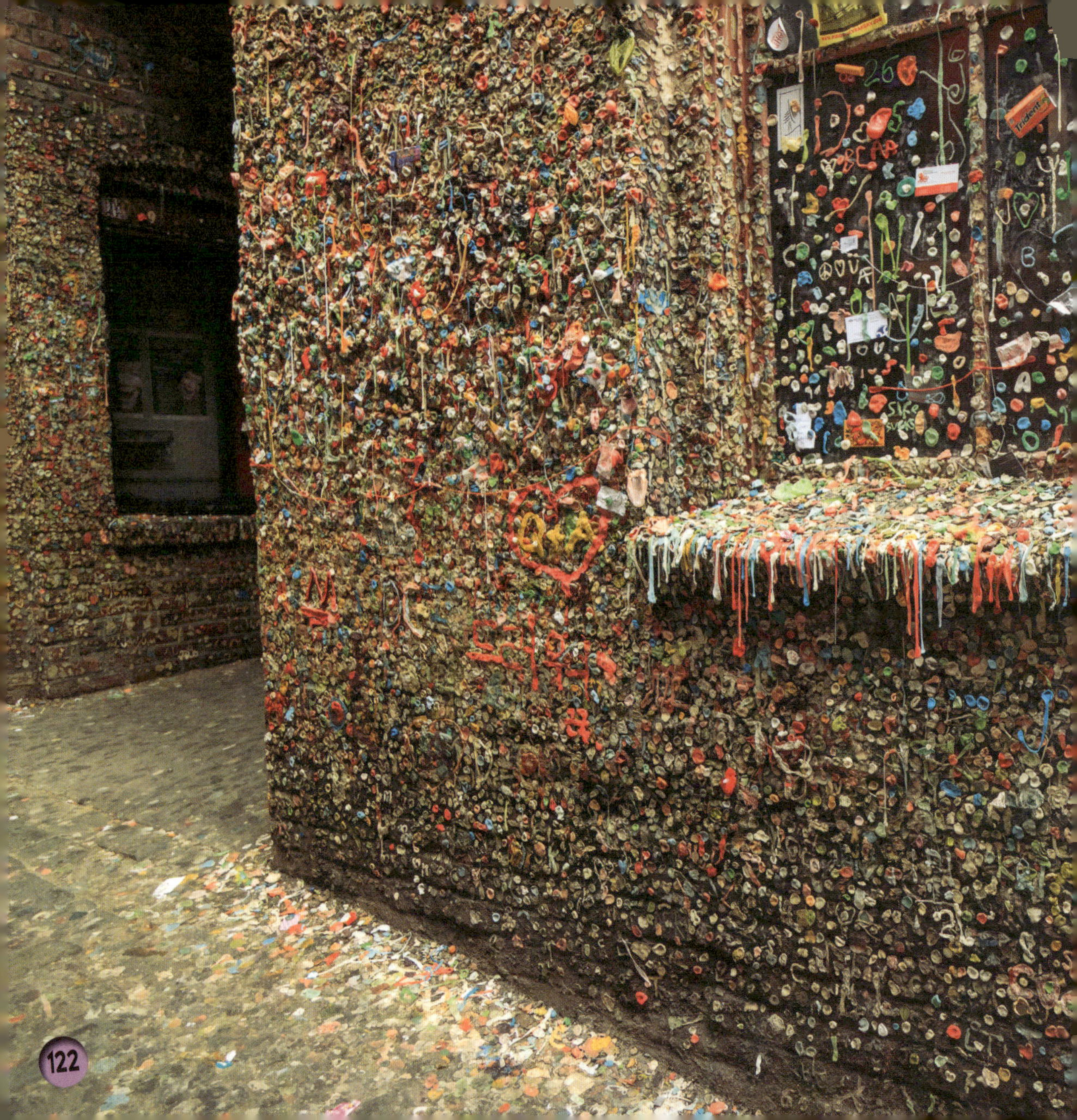
Trident

Sticky corner

Thousands of pieces of chewed gum have been stuck to a wall in Seattle, Washington.

Dolphins "name" each other by using unique **whistles.**

Big nose!

Stinky!

Sometimes the tuatara lizard of New Zealand breathes only **once an hour.**

Venezuela almost ran out of toilet paper in 2012.

WHOSE A PRETTY BOY THEN?

chuckle!

These bright pooches belong to Catherine Opson, a professional dog groomer from California.

I'm not leaving the house like this!

Time for your walk Sebastian!

CAN YOU FIGURE IT OUT?

Guess which body parts these odd-shaped vegetables look like?

A. Curvacious carrot

Ewww, get a bath!

B. Extraordinary eggplant

C. Curious cucumber

Answers: A: Legs B: Arms C: Mouth

Super Snails!

Twenty four snail sculptures made from recycled plastic were placed all around Sydney, Australia.

Are watermelons SQUARE?

Not usually, but in Japan they are sometimes grown in cubes so they stack better.

FLAME THROWER!

Anybody got a fire extinguisher?

132

Meet Fanny the world's largest walking robot! The robotic dragon measures 51 feet (16 m) long, has a wingspan of 40 feet (12 m), and can even breathe fire!

AMAZING ANTS

Ants started farming long before humans.

"Do the conga!"

Ants lived alongside the dinosaurs some 130 million years ago.

Ants form "supercolonies" that can stretch for thousands of miles.

LIGHT DELAY

It takes 8 minutes for sunlight to travel from the Sun to the Earth. This means if you see the Sun go out, it actually went out 8 minutes ago!

If you raise your legs slowly, and lie on your back, you can't sink in quicksand.

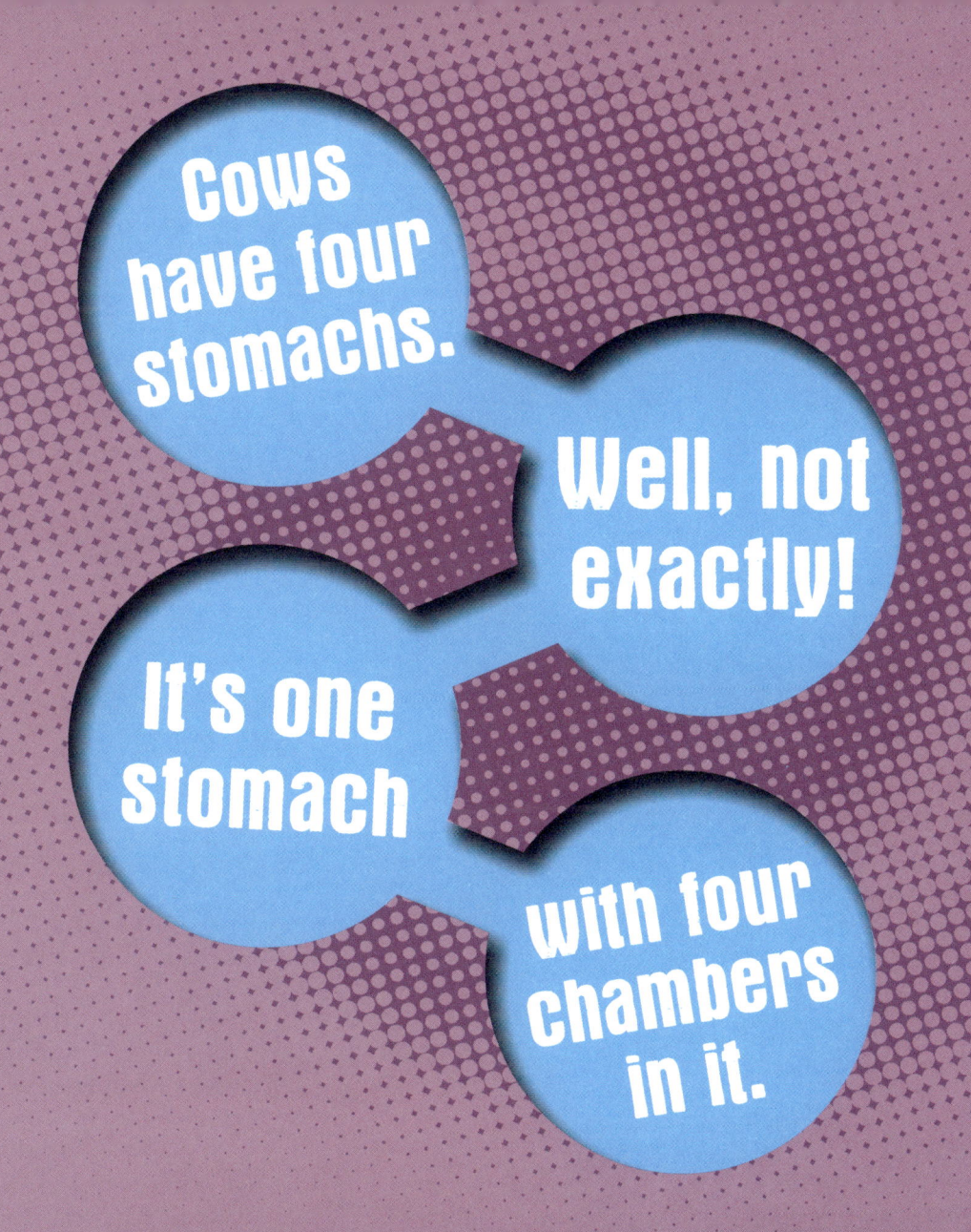

Cows have four stomachs. Well, not exactly! It's one stomach with four chambers in it.

"Get down" with the fishes

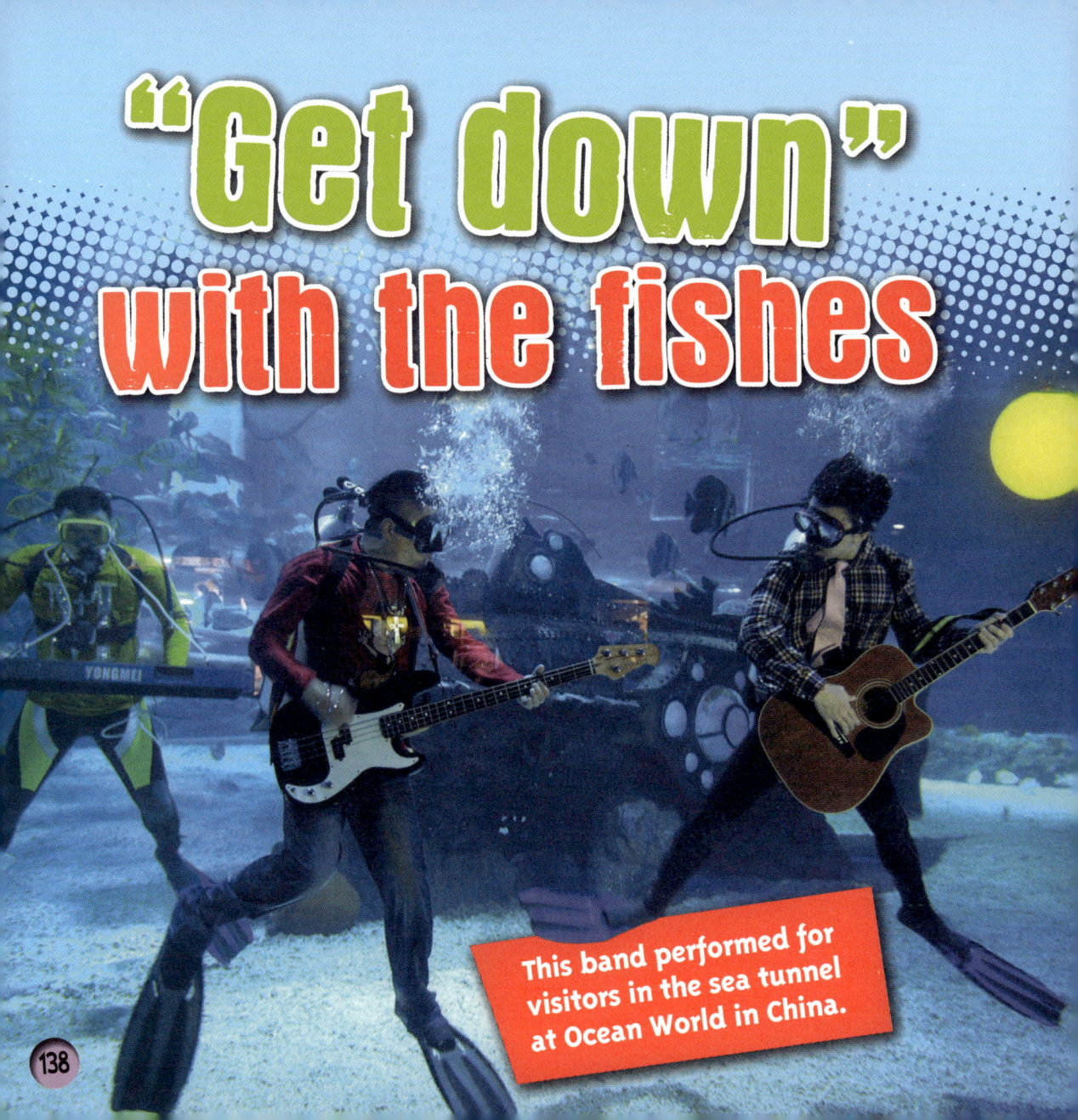

This band performed for visitors in the sea tunnel at Ocean World in China.

Mini monarch!

Would your majesty like her breakfast?

ZZZZZ...

Mary, Queen of Scots, became queen in 1542 when she was just SIX days old.

A dog has **220 million** smell receptors in its nose...

a rabbit has 100 million... you have just 5–6 million.

I can smell a rabbit!

Do thirsty plants scream?

If a plant is thirsty it will make a high-pitched sound, but it is too high for us to hear.

Eeeeeek!

Speak up!

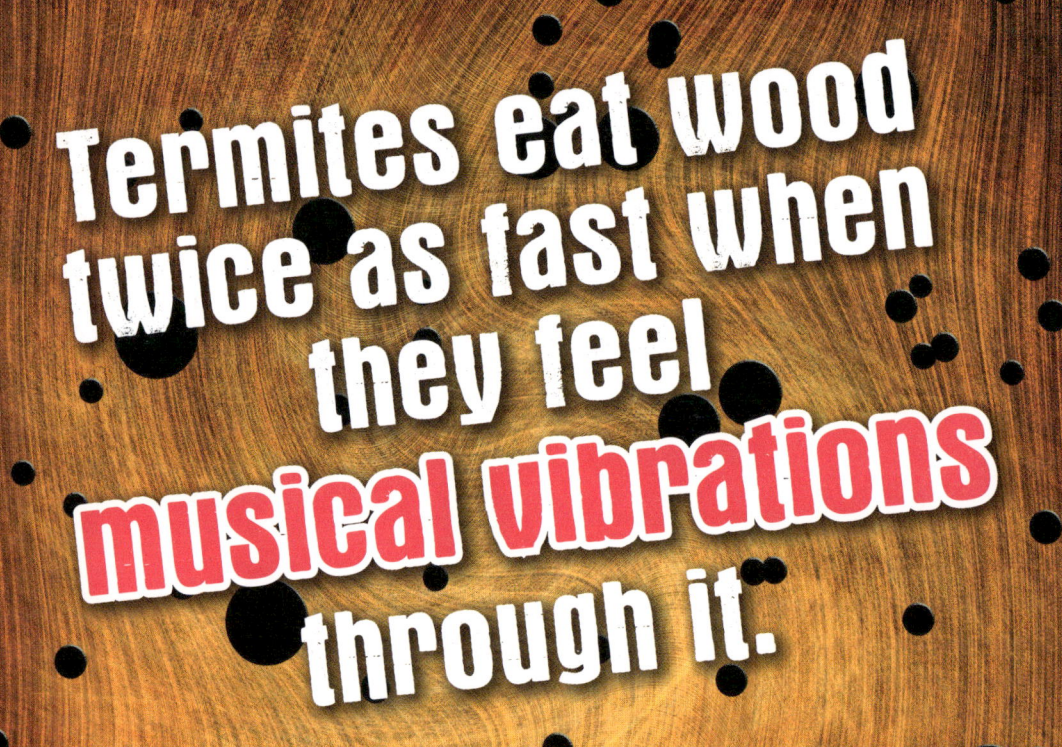

Termites eat wood twice as fast when they feel **musical vibrations** through it.

Cool, I love this tune!

"Wooden Heart" by Elvis?

Thorny devil lizards drink water through their **FEET.**

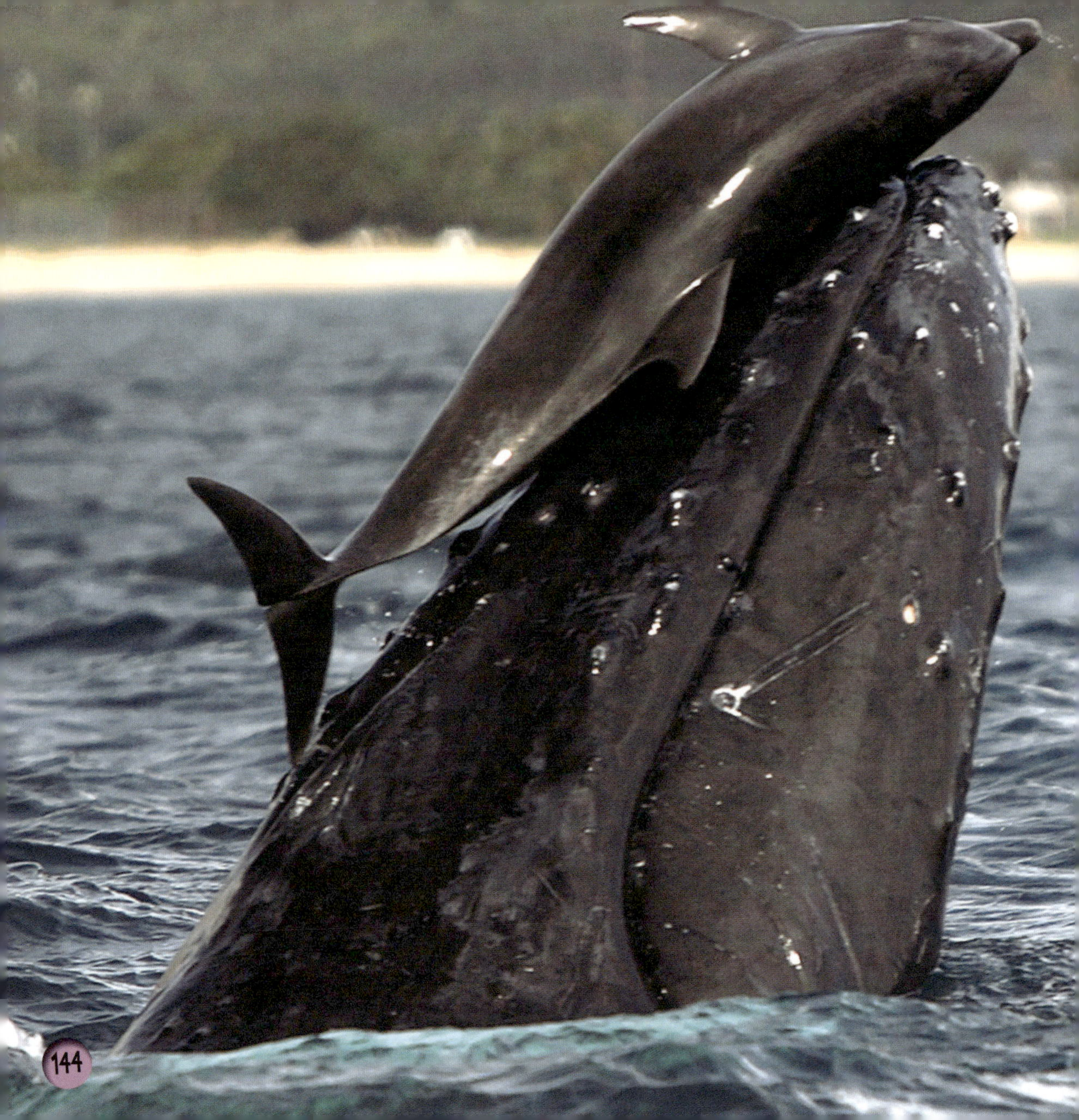

Yee Haa!

Bottlenose dolphins sometimes take rides on the heads of humpback whales.

SHREK LOOKALIKE!

This flower looks like Shrek the ogre! The rare bee orchid was found in Spain.

THREE BILLION PIZZAS

are sold in the U.S. every year — that's 350 slices

PER! SECOND!

BURP!

Q

Who asks over 400 questions a day?

A four-year-old child. Many of them are just "Why?"

Why? Leave it!

RAINBOW MAGIC

This tree in Hungary is covered in a rainbow of spiderweb crochet designs! Known as "Yarnbombing" the knitted webs took three months to stitch together!

FORK LIFT

Eat-Fit cutlery helps you exercise while eating! The knife and fork weigh 2 pounds (1 kg) each—the same as a bag of sugar—and the spoon is twice as heavy.

Try a "lighter" meal!

Little 'n' large

Einstein, a fourteen-inch-tall (36 cm) miniature horse, plays with Hannah, a St. Bernard dog!

Toy Plane?

I wonder what this switch does...

This plane is actually a kindergarten classroom! The plane, in the Georgian city of Rustavi, is full of desks, games and toys.

153

GOLD FACTS

An average human body contains **0.000007 ounces** (0.2 milligrams) of gold. That means you're worth about one cent!

All the gold mined in the world in a single year would **only fill the living room** in an average house.

Olympic gold medals contain only **1.3 percent gold.** They are actually 92.5 percent silver and the rest is copper.

Jumbo bunny

Ralph the giant rabbit weighs 56 pounds (25 kg) and measures three feet (1 m) in length.

OOOF!

Take a look at the size of those feet!

BZZZZZZZ

Whoa, headache!

Woodpeckers peck up to 20 times a second.

Hangin' around

Bats hang upside down because their legs are too weak to support their weight in an upright position.

YUMMY!

Americans started eating popcorn for breakfast in the 1800s.

Your head ages faster than your feet.

This is because time moves faster at higher levels, as the Earth's gravity is weaker up there.

Catching flies

Sticking out your tongue when you are concentrating helps your brain deal with information.

Careful though, you might catch a big, juicy fly!

MAY CONTAIN NUTS

yeah, she's nuts!

LillyBelle the dog has an amazing skill... she can sniff out nuts! She's been trained to find nuts and keep them away from seven-year-old Meghan Weingarth, who has a severe nut allergy.

Nuts!

LillyBelle raises her paw if any of Meghan's food contains nuts.

WHICH ANIMALS TIE THEIR TAILS TOGETHER?

Groups of South American Titi monkeys. Scientists think they do it as a sign of affection.

GUIDING STAR

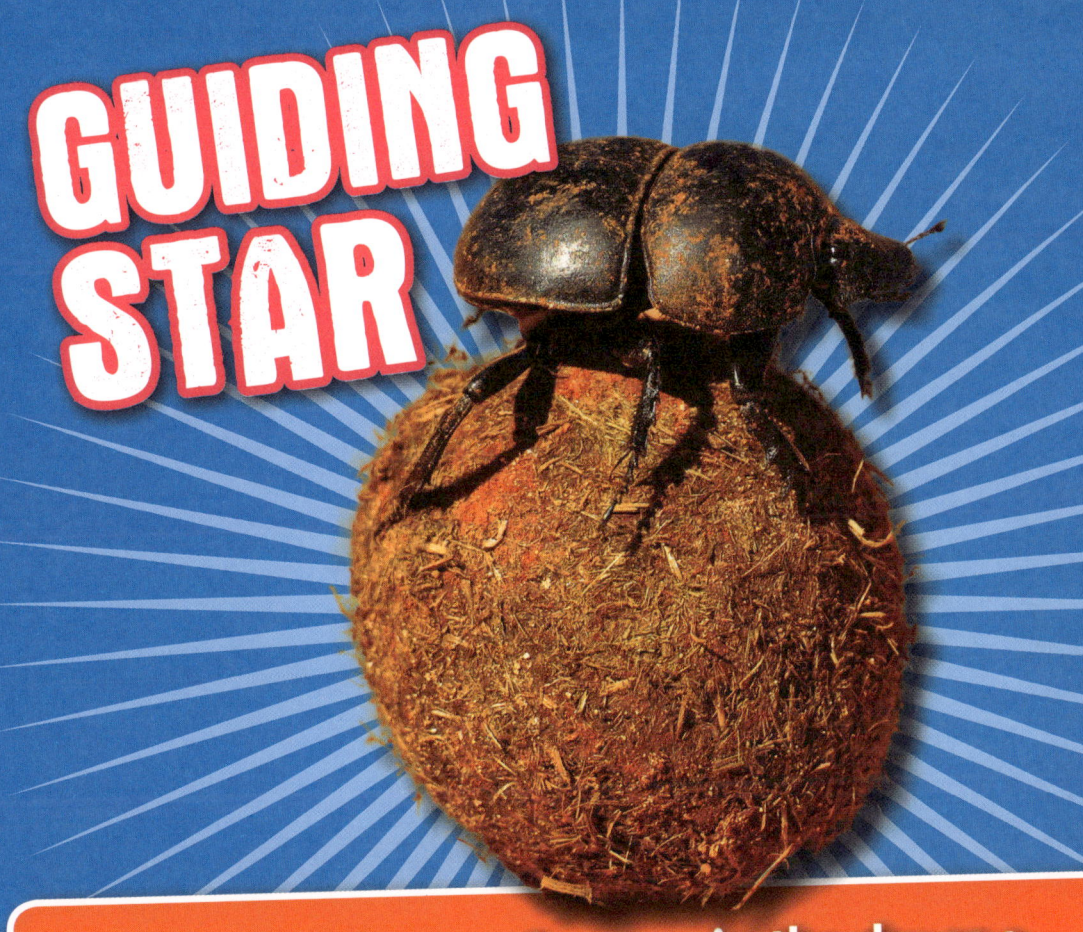

Dung beetles use the stars in the sky as a guide to help them move in straight lines at night. This stops them going round in circles.

NO WAY!

A woman in Boston paid $560,000 for two parking spaces in the city.

The worst game EVER!

Bokdrol Spoeg

is a South African sport where competitors spit antelope dung as far as possible.

That's just revolting!

Mr Stink!

Skunks can spray their smelly fluid as far as 15 feet (5 m).

oh yeh!

Censored!

charming!

LOOPY!

Aaron Homoki from Arizona completed a 15-foot-high (4.6-m) skateboard loop.

Wahoo!

Vincent van Goat

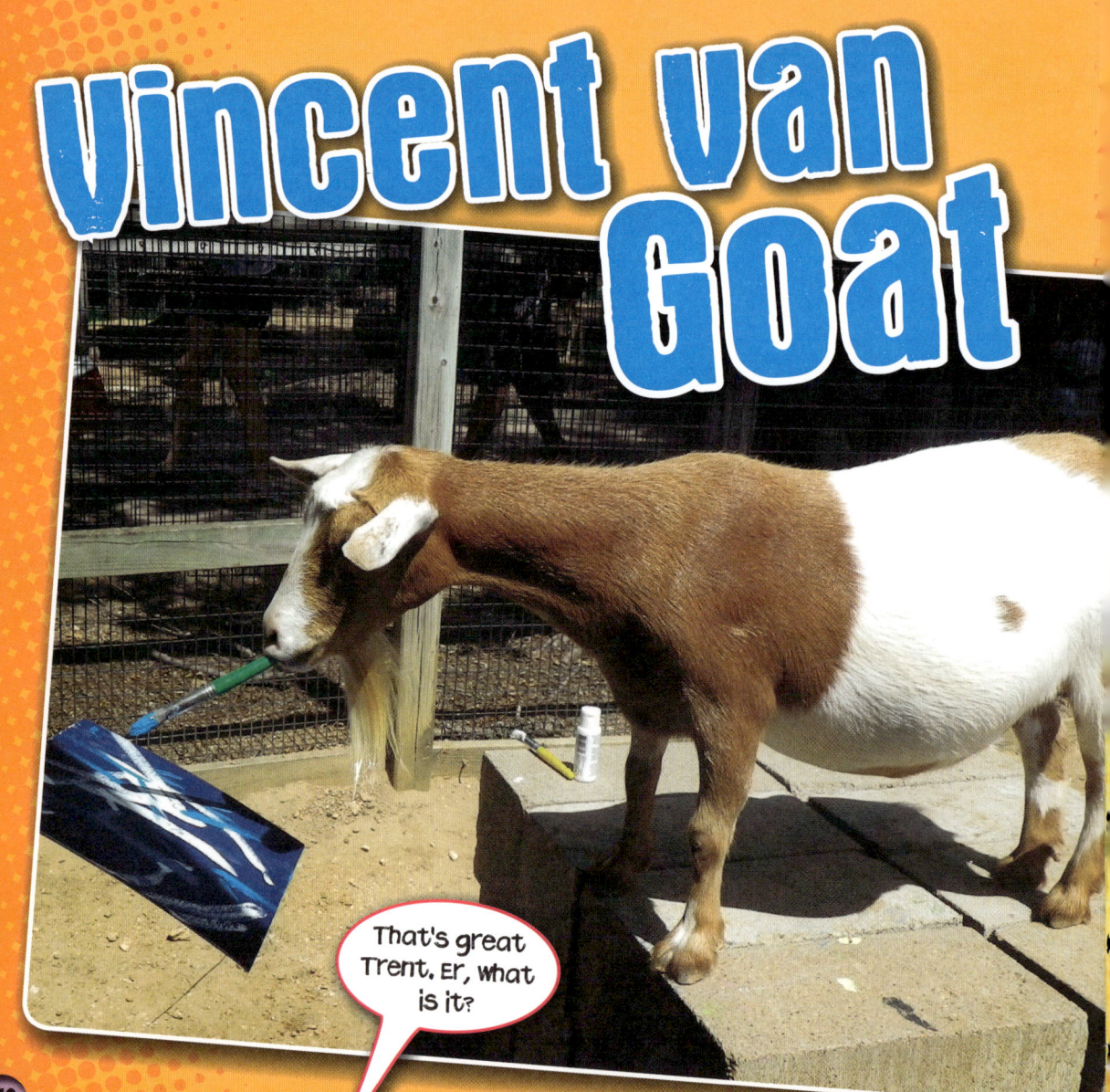

That's great Trent. Er, what is it?

Believe it or not, these are made of cake!

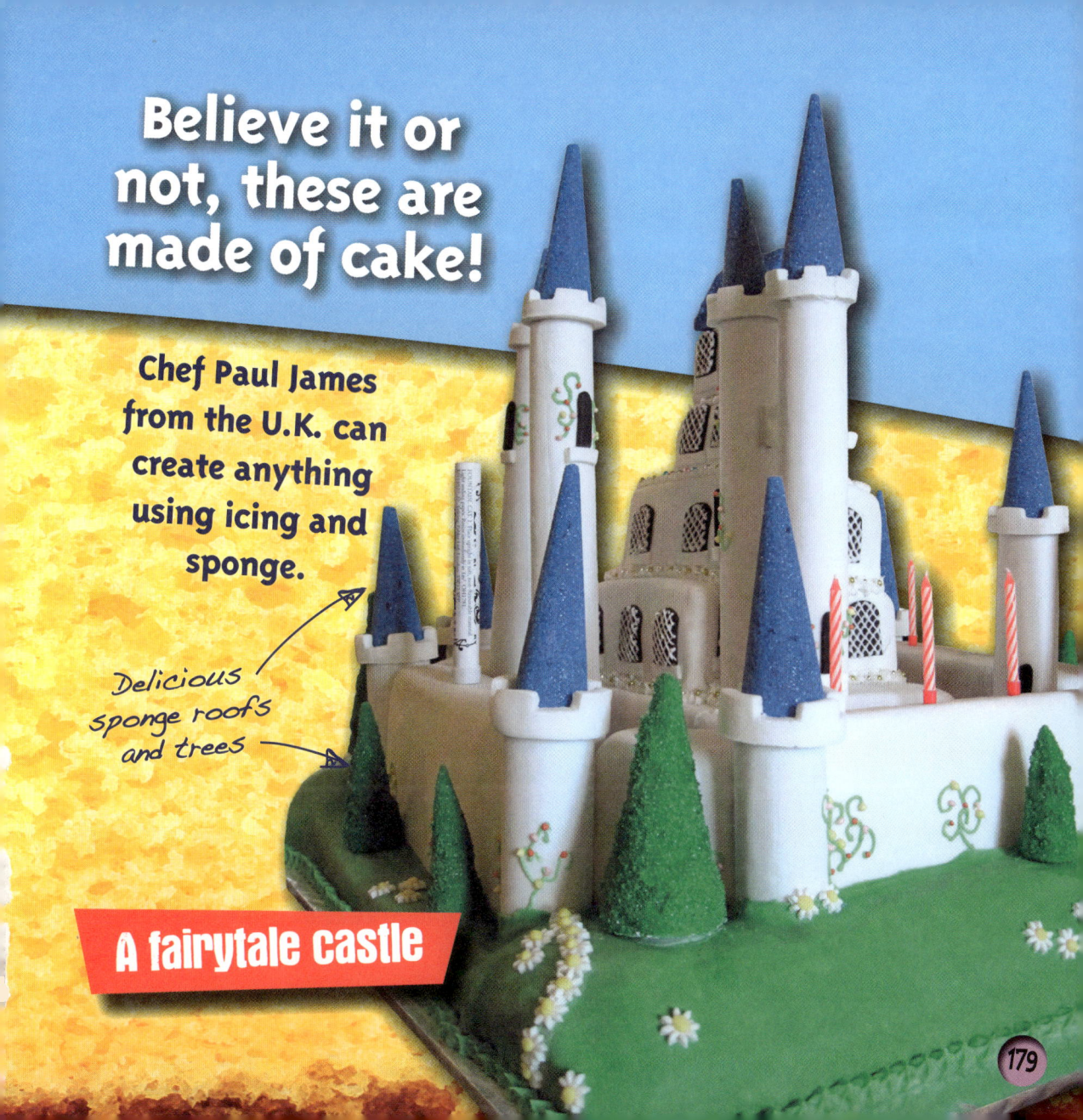

Chef Paul James from the U.K. can create anything using icing and sponge.

Delicious sponge roofs and trees

A fairytale castle

Longest lick?

Wow!

Giraffes clean their eyes and ears with their **21-inch** (53-cm) tongue.

Counting one billion seconds would take you about **31.7 years**.

Er, don't try it!

Some bees in Thailand drink HUMAN TEARS.

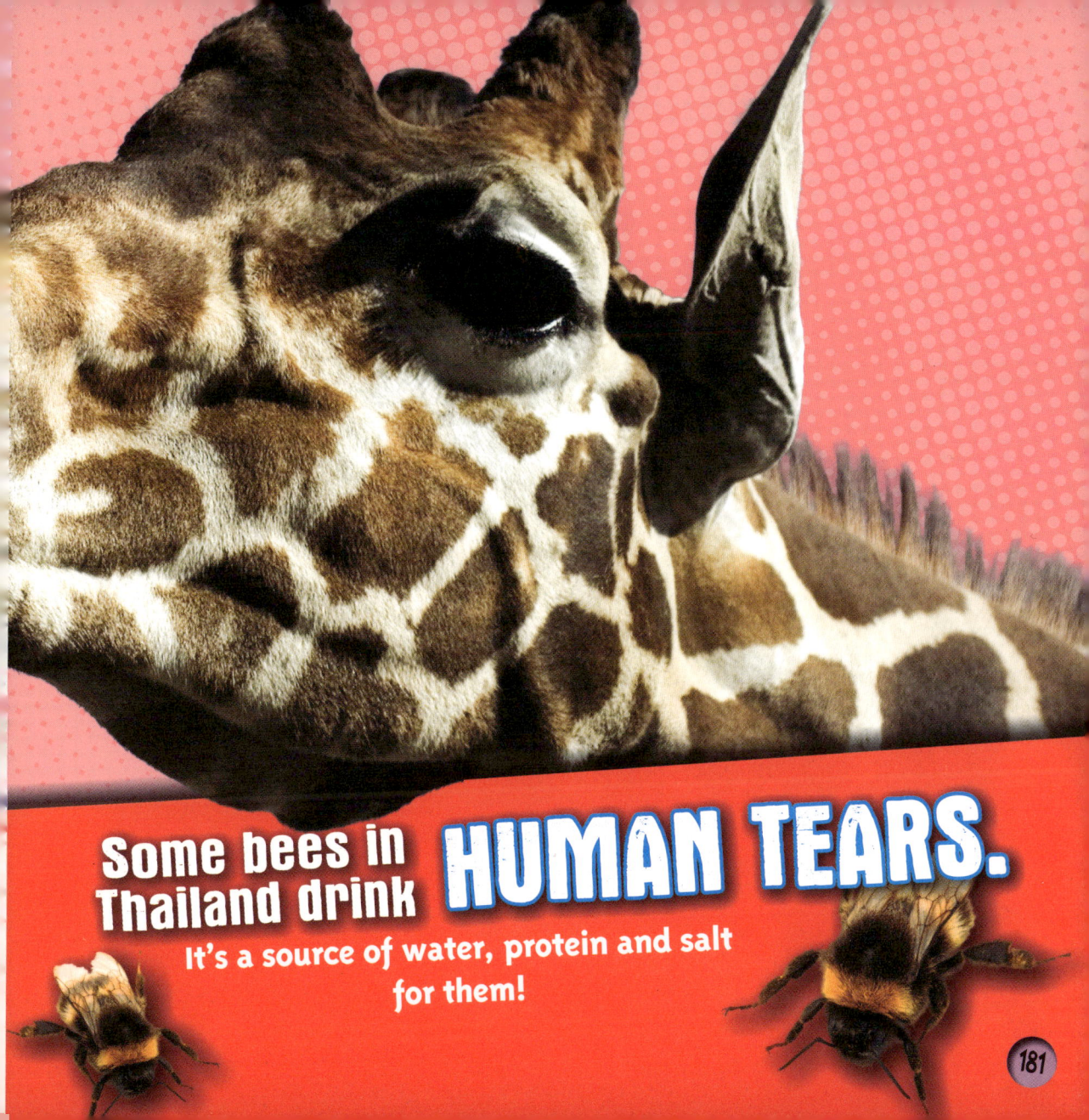

It's a source of water, protein and salt for them!

The pilot and co-pilot on a plane always eat different meals.

If they were both to get sick from food poisoning there would be no one to fly the plane!

SLOPPY CHOPS!

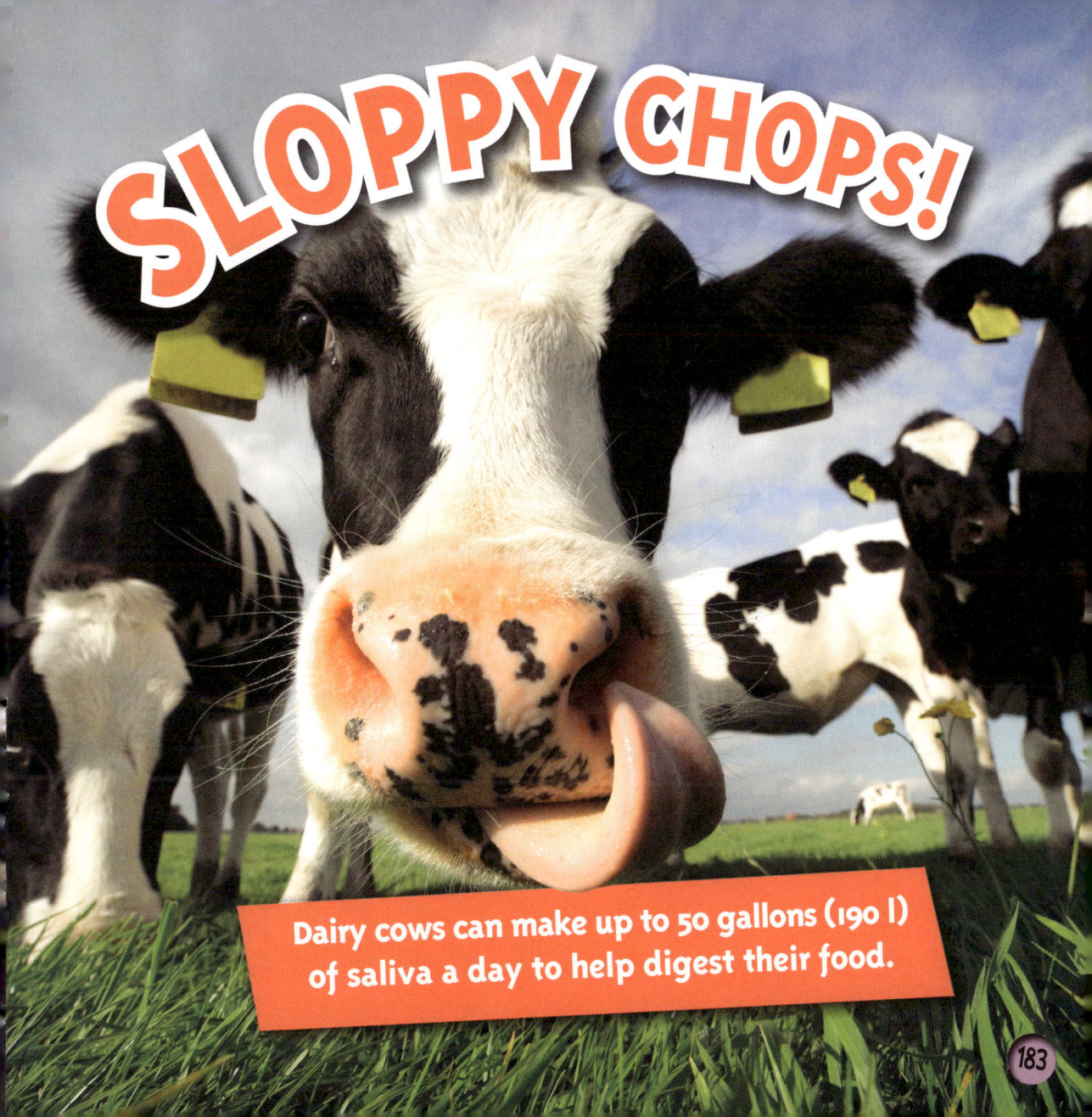

Dairy cows can make up to 50 gallons (190 l) of saliva a day to help digest their food.

184

Choc Frock

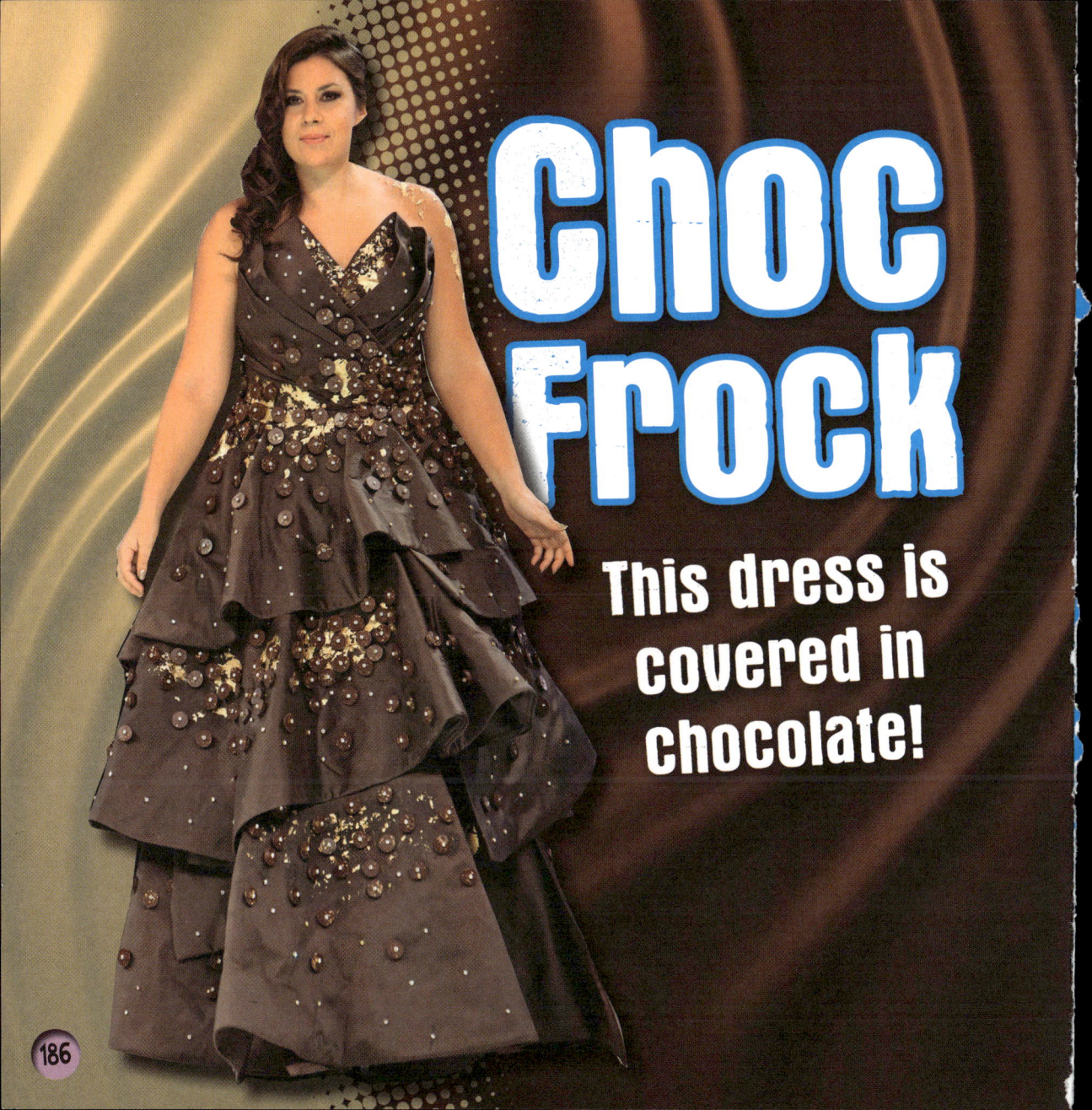

This dress is covered in chocolate!

ERASER EXTRAVAGANZA

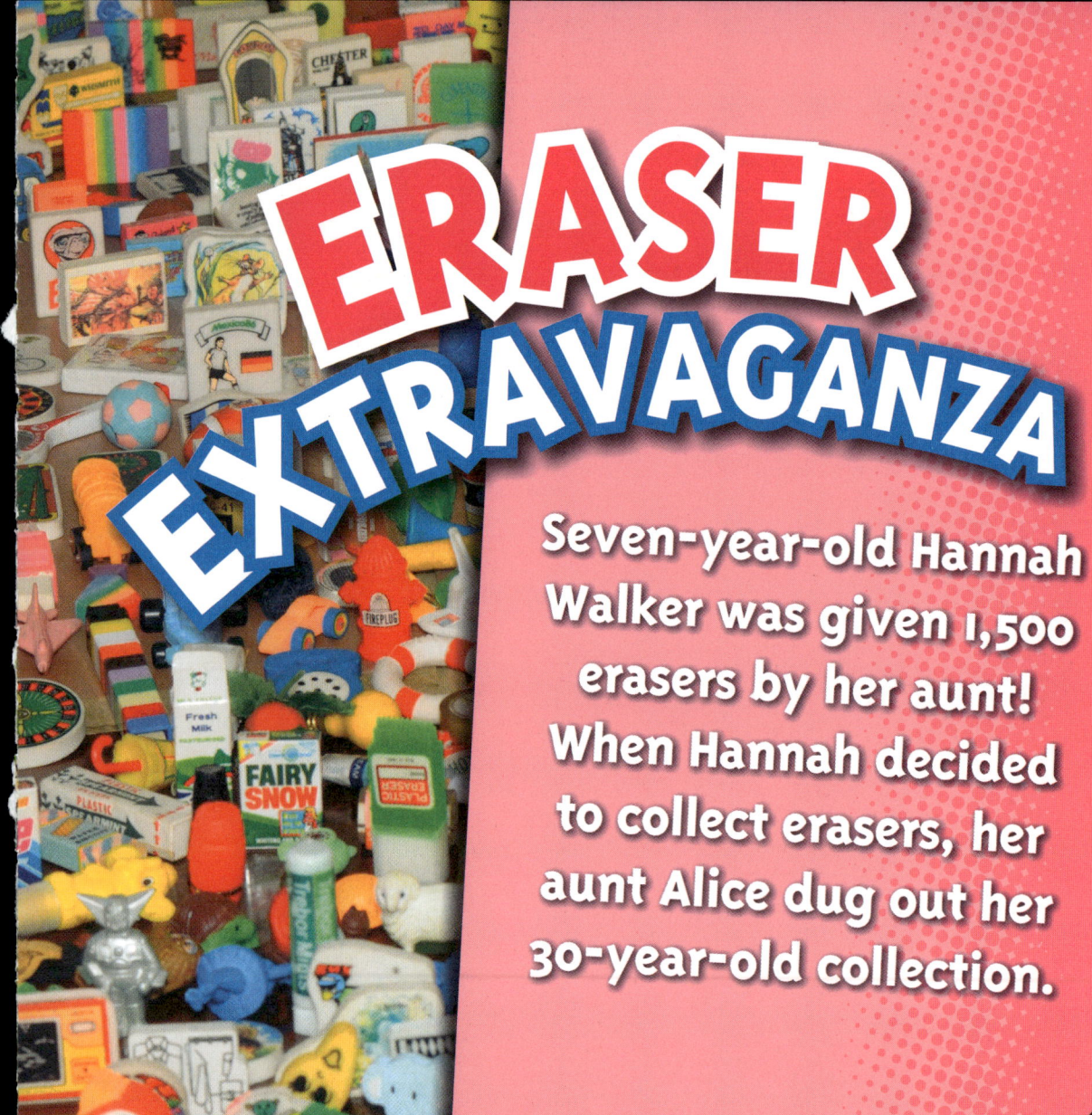

Seven-year-old Hannah Walker was given 1,500 erasers by her aunt! When Hannah decided to collect erasers, her aunt Alice dug out her 30-year-old collection.

What has 750 legs but is only 1.2 inches (3 cm) long?

A female millipede from California.

Chocolate, in the form of cacao beans, was used as money until the late 19th century in parts of South America.

The average chocolate bar has about **8 insects' legs** in it.

what?

Scientists think that if you lived on Earth 1,900 million years ago, it would have smelled like **rotten eggs.**

Snakes smell with their tongue.

Horsemaid

"Get off me foot!"

Alex Wells from the U.K. had her horse Toffee as one of her bridesmaids on her wedding day.

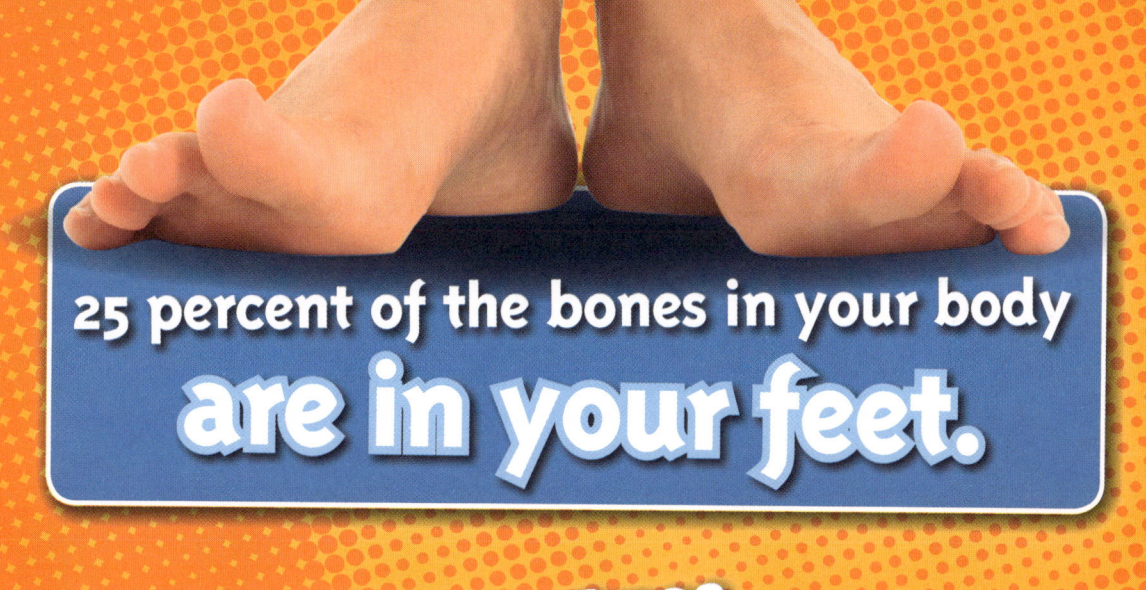

25 percent of the bones in your body **are in your feet.**

Lightning is five times **HOTTER** than the surface of the Sun.

CAUGHT YOU!

How embarrassing!

Some seals in Norway have red faces!

The iron particles in the sea can stick to the hairs on their face causing it to turn red.

yes, and you've got nothing on!

Salamanders use their lungs to hear sounds!

You would have **33,554,432** direct ancestors... if you traced your family tree back 25 generations.

WATER MUSIC

OK, who stole my guitar?

This surfer, dressed as a rock star, competes in the ZJ Boarding House Halloween Surf Contest in California.

Aaron Bling can hold a note on his saxophone for 39 minutes 40 seconds.

LOVE AND FLEECE

"Hi man!"

Long-haired sheep Bobbie Marley has curly dreadlocks!

An average person grows **590 miles** (950 km) of hair in a lifetime!

Which animal has see-through blood?

The ocellated ice fish.

Some farmers in Africa use

HOT!...

chili peppers

to keep elephants away from their crops.

Lightning strikes the Earth about **8 million** times a day.

An average person will walk the same as four times around the Earth during their lifetime.

Only 1 percent of the water on Earth is drinkable.

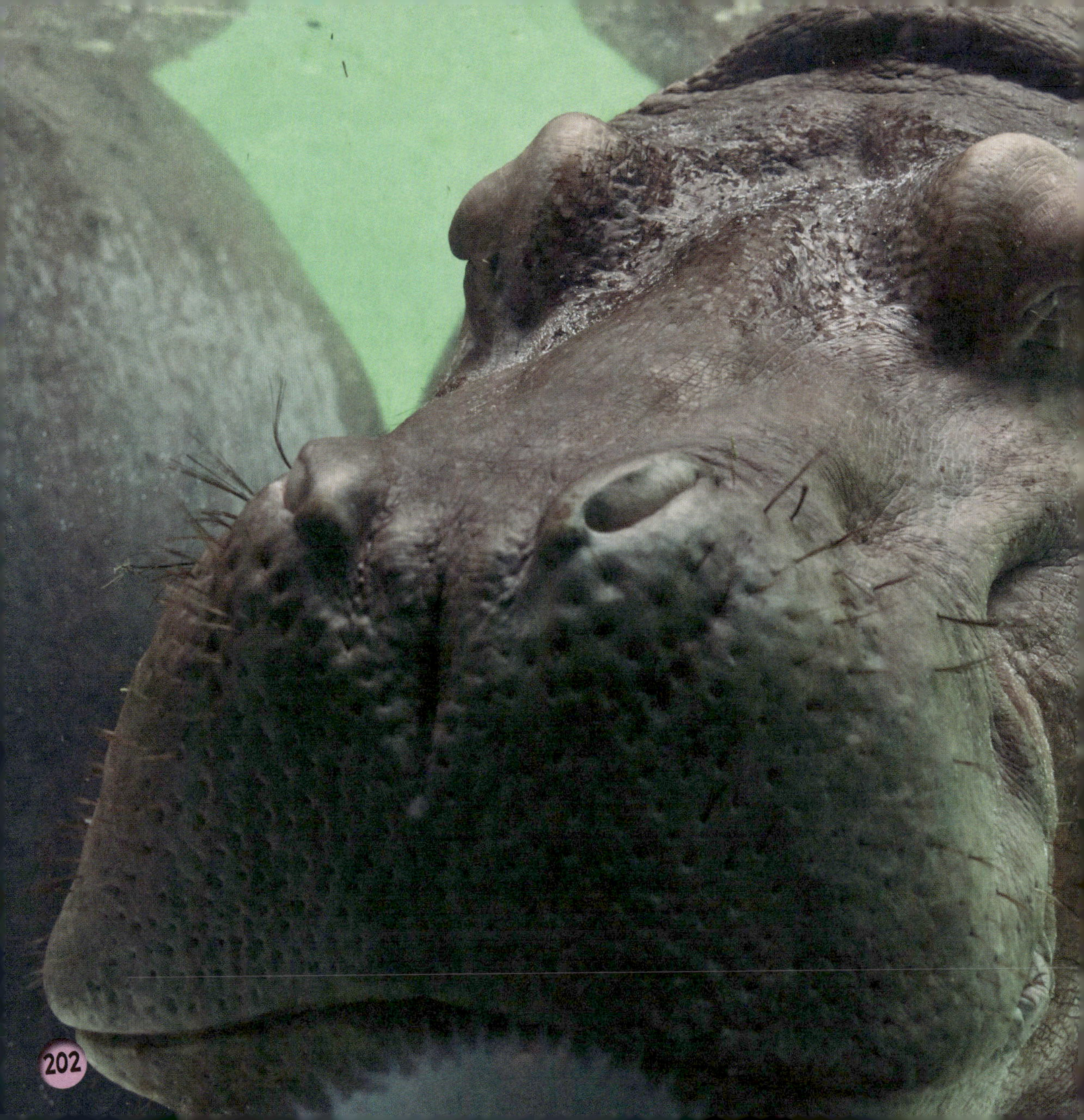

OUT COLD!

Hippos sleep underwater. They rise to the surface to breathe without waking.

STRANGE CARGO

The first passengers in a hot-air balloon were a sheep, a duck and a rooster.

They flew from Versailles, France, in 1783.

I think we're gonna crash!

It's OK for you two, you can fly anyway!

SNOW BOATS

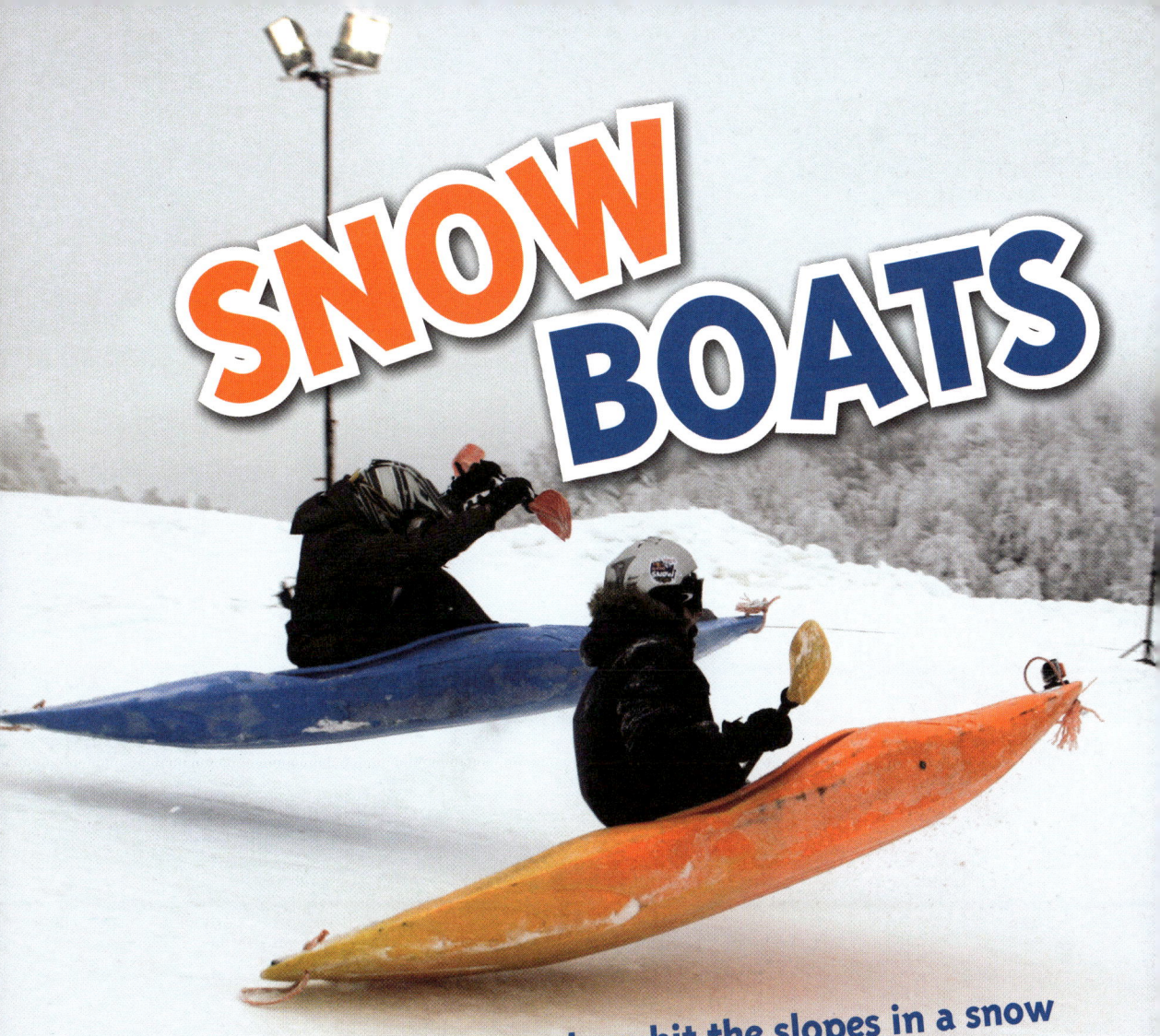

Kayakers hit the slopes in a snow boat downhill race in Estonia.

CHRISTMAS COLLECTION

Sylvia Pope from the U.K. has a collection of more than 1,750 Christmas decorations.

207

Can you roll your tongue into a tube?

At least 65 percent of the population can.

HOT PANDA

Wei Wei the panda cooled down in summer by hugging a giant ice block!

Ahhhhh!

DOG DUDES

Surfing dogs compete in the Surf City Surf Dog competition in Huntington Beach, California.

The wipe out...

...as we see the front of the board start to go under, disaster is just moments away—and he knows it!

Text book

Cool, calm and collected. Way to go!

The doggie double

Nicely done, although "number 2" seems to be having a hard time—maybe it's the view?

A praying mantis can turn its head **ALL THE WAY AROUND.**

It is the only insect that can do this.

I do suffer from neck ache in the mornings though.

A blue whale has enough air

Huff.

in its lungs to fill about
2,500 balloons!

FLAMIN' TUBA

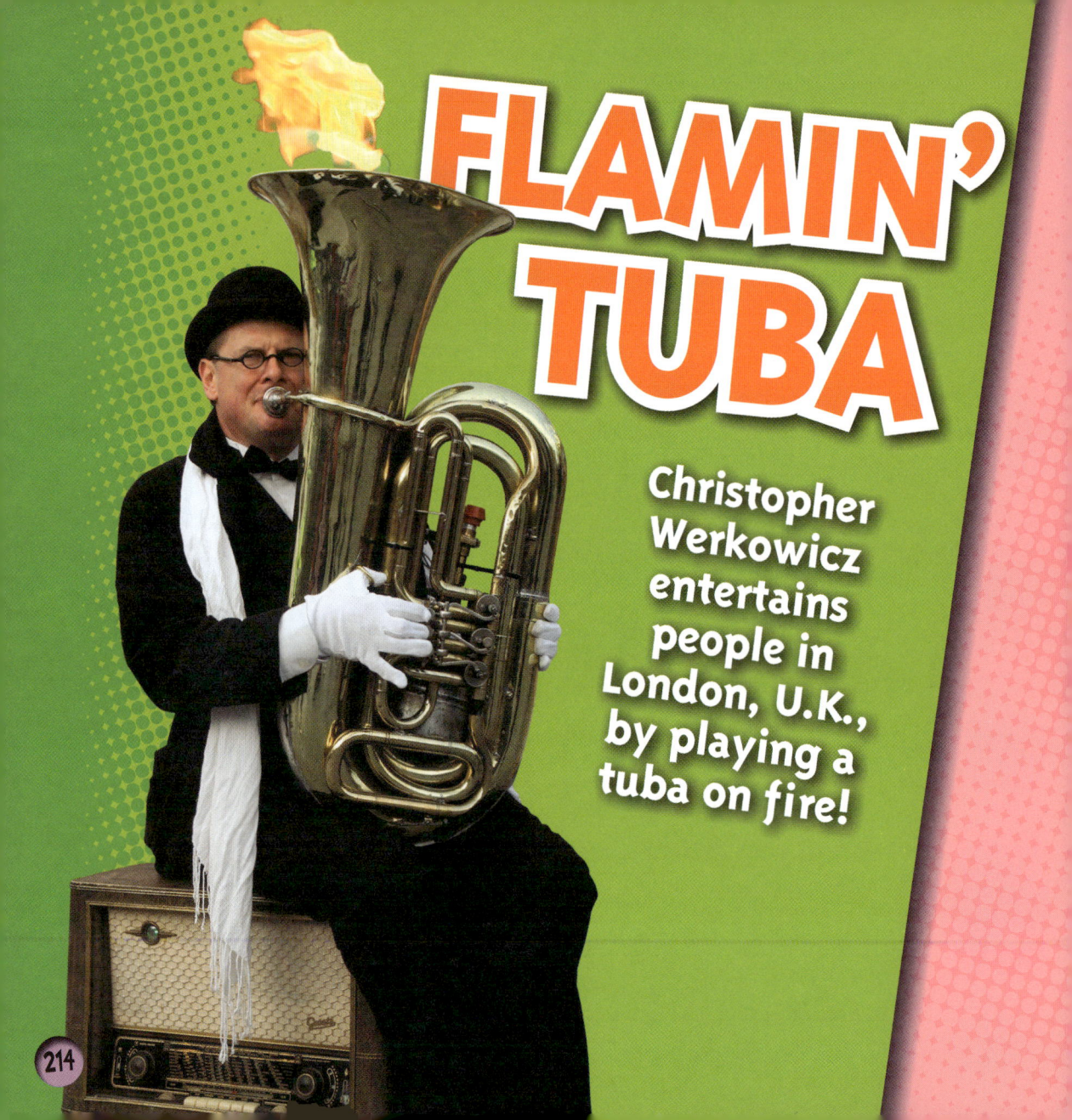

Christopher Werkowicz entertains people in London, U.K., by playing a tuba on fire!

Your **left lung** is smaller than your **right lung** to make room for your **heart.**

215

BAD HAIR DAY?

An ancient Roman hair dye formula included **pickled leeches, sea urchins and lard.**

Your thigh bones are stronger than concrete.

CLINK

Rope climbing was an Olympic sport until 1932.

More than half of the world's population has never made or received a phone call.

Anybody there?

CAT BURGLAR!

Norris the cat creeps out at night and steals clothes, slippers and food from nearby houses! He sneaks in through cat flaps and comes home the next morning with the stolen goods. He has even taken a bath mat and towel set!

INDEX

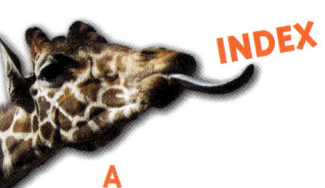

A
airports 79
ancestors 194
Antarctica 55, 95
anteaters 60
ants 55, 134–135
apples 41
art 20–21, 44–45, 170–171
astronauts 100, 112

B
baboons 8–9
baldness 94
balloons 97, 105, 204, 213
bats 158
bears 52–53, 174
bees 181
beetles 165
bicycles 18–19, 116
blood 58, 198
bones 191, 217
brains 22, 111, 119
breathing 83, 124
bubble soccer 104
butterflies 109

C
cakes 178–179
cars 102, 166, 175
cats 28, 48–49, 74, 219
caves 120
chewing gum 59, 122–123
chicken 94, 204
chimpanzees 52–53
chocolate 111, 118–119, 186–187
Christmas 98, 206–207

clothes 79, 186
cows 103, 121, 137, 183
crabs 72
crochet 149
crocodiles 42–43
cutlery 150

D
dinosaurs 135
dogs 6–7, 62–63, 95, 126–127, 140, 151, 162–163, 176–177, 210–211
dolphins 124, 144–145
dragons 132–133
drinking 67, 143
ducks 106–107, 204
dung throwing 167

E
ears 109, 119
Earth 200–201
eggs 189
elephants 47, 68, 80–81, 82, 102, 199
Empire State Building 66
erasers 184–185
eyes 118

F
family trees 194
feet 143, 160, 191
fire engines 64
fish 50–51, 73, 88, 96, 110, 198
flamingos 4–5
flying 24–25, 116
fruit 46, 54, 71, 117, 131

G
genes 117
gerbils 38
giraffes 180–181

glabella 108
goats 170–171
gold 154–155
gostra 39
gravity 160

H
hair 198, 216
hamsters 38
hands 118
heads 160
hearts 37, 96, 119, 215
height 100
hippos 202–203
horses 83, 86–87, 151, 190

I
ice 110

K
kangaroos 65
kayaks 205
kidneys 118
kindergarten 152–153

L
Las Vegas 109
laughing 65
leeches 216
lightning 191, 200
Little Miss 56–57
livers 118
lizards 84, 124, 143
lungs 40, 119, 194, 213, 215
lying 85

M
mascots 34–35
mice 36, 38
millipedes 188

220

money 173, 187
monkeys 8–9, 10–11, 52–53, 164
monsters 16–17
mosquitos 120
Mr. Men 56–57
music 15, 138, 142, 195, 196, 214

N
noses 85, 103
numbers 180
nuts 162–163

O
Olympics 155, 217
orangutans 10–11
orchids 146
oxygen 70

P
painting 170–171
pandas 78, 209
parking spaces 166
penguins 74, 92–93
pigs 14, 22, 30–31
pizzas 147
planes 89, 152–153, 182
poop 94, 167
popcorn 159
praying mantis 212

Q
queens 139
quicksand 136

R
rabbits 91, 140, 156
rain 114
rats 69
rattlesnakes 66
robots 132–133

Rock, Paper, Scissors
  Championships 76–77
rope climbing 217
rubber ducks 106–107

S
salamanders 194
saliva 183
sandwiches 16–17
Santa Claus 95
saxophones 196
seals 192–193
senses 112, 140
sheep 101, 172, 197, 204
skateboards 169
skunks 168
sleep 59, 86–87, 113, 202–203
smelling 120, 140
snails 130
snakes 66, 189
sneezing 96
snoring 113
snow 115, 205
space 100, 112
spiders 66
squid 36–37
stomachs 137
street art 20–21
the Sun 136, 191
surfing 195, 210–211
swans 88
swimming 72, 80–81

T
tadpoles 61
tails 164
tears 181
teddy bears 174
telephones 218
television 176–177

termites 142
thirst 141
thorny devils 143
tickling 69
tigers 12–13, 14
toilet paper 125
tongues 60, 84, 161, 180–181, 189, 208
trees 55, 70, 149
Trevi fountain 173
tubas 214
twyndyllyngs 99

V
Valentine's Day 41
vegetables 44–45, 58–59, 128–129, 199
vending machines 90
Venezuela 125
VW Beetles 175

W
walking 201
water 67, 173, 201
waterbucks 74
weddings 190
whales 82, 144–145, 213
woodlice 113
woodpeckers 157
worms 32, 78

Y
"Yarnbombing" 149

PHOTO CREDITS

COVER www.firebox.com (front); © Szente A – Shutterstock.com (back)

4-5 © Anna Omelchenko – Shutterstock.com; **6-7** Le Petite Maison/Solent News/Rex; **8-9** Tanya Stollznow/Solent News/Rex; **10-11** Barry Bland/Rex; **14** Reuters/Sukree Sukplang SS/TW; **16-17** Caters News Agency; **18-19** Reuters/Fabrizio Bensch; **20-21** Reuters/Robert Pratta; **22** EPA; **23** Alex Mitt – Shutterstock.com; **24-25** Reuters/Maxim Shemetov; **26** Eyepress/Abhisek Saha/Sipa/Rex; **27** (t) Reuters/Dinuka Liyanawatte, (b) Reuters/Marko Djurica; **28** © Irina oxilixo Danilova – Shutterstock.com; **30-31** Steve Hill/Rex; **32** © Kletr – Shutterstock.com; **33** © Xavier DeMarco – Shutterstock.com; **34-35** Koichi Nakamura/AP/Press Association Images; **36** (b) © kontur-vid – Shutterstock.com; **38** Central Garden and Pet; **39** Reuters/Darrin Zammit Lupi; **40** © DeanHarty – Shutterstock.com; **41** Quirky China News/Rex; **42-43** © Mark McEwan/naturepl.com; **44-45** Reuters/China Daily; **47** © CoolKengzz – Shutterstock.com; **48-49** Goldtatze/Rex; **50-51** Daniel Trimm/Rex; **52-53** Barry Bland/Rex; **54** HAP/Quirky China News/Rex; **55** © rodho – Shutterstock.com; **56-57** Joanne Black; **60** © Eric Isselee – Shutterstock.com; **61** © luchschen – Shutterstock.com; **62-63** Cushzilla/Bournemouth News/Rex; **64** Geoffrey Robinson/Rex; **65** © Eric Isselee – Shutterstock.com; **67** © PavleMarjanovic – Shutterstock.com; **68** © Regien Paassen – Shutterstock.com; **69** © Pakhnyushcha – Shutterstock.com; **70** (c) © Perig – Shutterstock.com, (b) © Lisa F. Young – Shutterstock.com; **71** (c) © Valentina Proskurina – Shutterstock.com, (b/r) © Zygotehaasnobrain – Shutterstock.com; **72** © Pan Xunbin – Shutterstock.com; **74** (l) Sue Flood/Caters News, (r) Nancie Wight/Nat Geo Creative/Caters News; **75** Johan Van Berkel/Caters News; **76-77** Caters News Agency; **78** © aleksandr hunta – Shutterstock.com; **79** © monticello – Shutterstock.com; **80-81** Bournemouth News/Rex; **84** © ladyphoto – Shutterstock.com; **85** © Insago – Shutterstock.com; **86-87** © Rita Kockmarjova – Shutterstock.com; **88** Reuters/China Daily; **89** © B747 – Shutterstock.com; **91** © Eric Isselee – Shutterstock.com; **92-93** Ben Cranke/naturepl.com; **94** © Ilya Akinshin – Shutterstock.com; **96** © wavebreakmedia – Shutterstock.com; **97** Shimon Mentel/Solent News/Rex; **98** Reuters/Michaela Rehle; **99** © stockyimages – Shutterstock.com; **100** © siraphat – Shutterstock.com; **101** © Traveler – Shutterstock.com; **102** © Georgy Markov – Shutterstock.com; **103** Jorge Casais – Shutterstock.com; **104** Daniel Reinhardt/DPA/Press Association Images; **105** (c) © montego – Shutterstock.com, (bgd) © Vereschchagin Dmitry – Shutterstock.com; **106-107** © Picture Alliance/Photoshot; **108** © Timothy Boomer – Shutterstock.com; **111** Inition/Rex Features; **112** © ArchMan – Shutterstock.com; **113** © Mauro Rodrigues – Shutterstock.com; **116** Jonathan Hordle/Rex; **117** (b) © WEExp – Shutterstock.com; (c) © Hong Vo – Shutterstock.com; **118-119** Chocolate by Mueller; **121** © biletskiy – Shutterstock.com; **122-123** © Stuart Westmorland/Corbis; **124** © Alex James Bramwell – Shutterstock.com; **126-127** Reuters/Mike Blake; **128** Israel Gruber; **129** (t) Landon Martino, (b) Gabe Brown; **130** Jin Linpeng/Landov/Press Association Images; **132-133** Supplied by Wenn.com; **134-135** © Andrey Armyagov – Shutterstock.com; **136** © losw – Shutterstock.com; **138** © Xinhua/Photoshot; **139** © Natalia Kirichenko – Shutterstock.com.

140 © Roland Ijdema - Shutterstock.com; 141 © Zeljko Radojko - Shutterstock.com; 142 © argus - Shutterstock.com; 144-145 SeaPics.com; 146 © David Chapman/ardea.com; 147 © Microstock Man - Shutterstock.com; 149 Babukatorium/Solent News/Rex; 150 Solent News/Rex; 151 Reuters; 152-153 Vano Shlamov/AFP/Getty Images; 156 M & Y News Ltd/Rex; 157 © Brian Lasenby - Shutterstock.com; 158 © Super Prin - Shutterstock.com; 159 © Vitaly Korovin - Shutterstock.com; 160 (t) © Instudio 68 - Shutterstock.com, (b) © SvetlanaFedoseyeva - Shutterstock.com; 161 © djem - Shutterstock.com; 162-163 Caters News Agency; 165 © john michael evan potter - Shutterstock.com; 166 © Neale Cousland - Shutterstock.com; 168 © Ultrashock - Shutterstock.com; 169 Reuters/Mike Blake; 170-171 Caters News Agency; 174 © Bara22 - Shutterstock.com; 175 Andy Wilsheer/Rex; 176-177 © Erik Lam - Shutterstock.com; 178-179 Paul James/Solent News/Rex; 180-181 © Szente A - Shutterstock.com; 181 © Allocricetulus - Shutterstock.com; 182 © Ivica Drusany - Shutterstock.com; 183 © Sebastian Knight - Shutterstock.com; 184-185 Mike Walker/Rex; 186 David Silpa/Landov/Press Association Images; 187 © Preto Perola - Shutterstock.com; 188-189 © Eric Isselee - Shutterstock.com; 189 © Evgeny Karandaev - Shutterstock.com; 190 Caters News Agency; 191 © Viachaslau Kraskouski - Shutterstock.com; 192-193 Hank Perry/ Solent News/Rex; 194 (t) © Alhovik - Shutterstock.com, (b) © filfoto - Shutterstock.com; 195 Reuters/Lucy Nicholson; 197 Richard Austin/Rex; 199 © Maks Narodenko - Shutterstock.com; 201 © leonello calvetti - Shutterstock.com; 202-203 © Lovingyou2911 - Shutterstock.com; 205 Reuters/Ints Kalnins; 206 © DenisNata - Shutterstock.com; 206-207 Rex; 208 © Ozugur Coskun - Shutterstock.com; 209 EPA/STR, Camera Press London; 210-211 Reuters/Lucy Nicholson; 212 © Jiang Hongyan - Shutterstock.com; 213 © Nature Art - Shutterstock.com; 214 © David Mbiyu/Demotix/Corbis; 216 de2marco - Shutterstock.com; 217 (l) © dream designs - Shutterstock.com, (r) © Nomad_Soul - Shutterstock.com; 218 © Aaron Amat - Shutterstock.com; 219 Swns.com

Key: t = top, b = bottom, c = center, l = left, r = right, bgd = background

All other photos are from Ripley Entertainment Inc. and Shutterstock.com. Every attempt has been made to acknowledge correctly and contact copyright holders and we apologize in advance for any unintentional errors or omissions, which will be corrected in future editions.

Have you seen books one and two? They're packed with even more fun facts and silly stories!

We hope you enjoyed the book!

If you have a fun fact or silly story, why not email us at bionresearch@ripleys.com or write to us at BION Research, Ripley Entertainment Inc., 7576 Kingspointe Parkway, Suite 188, Orlando, Florida 32819, U.S.A.